NILE REFLECTIONS

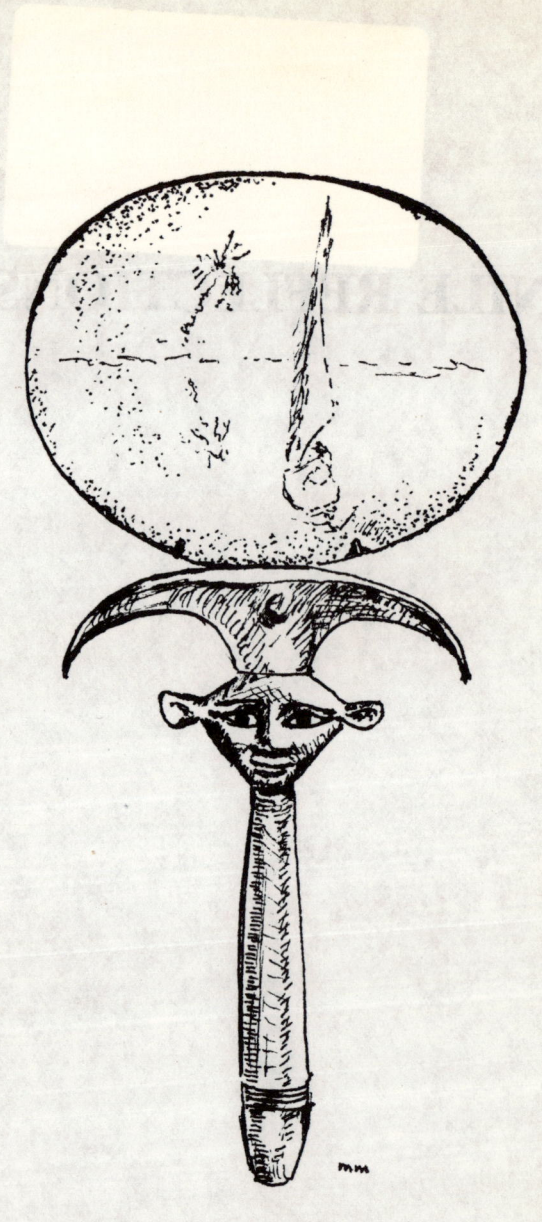

NILE REFLECTIONS

An Anthology of Broadcasts, Articles and Essays, 1946 - 1986

by
DOREEN ANWAR

With illustrations
by
Marion Miller Moharram

By the same author: *We Live and Remember, the story of NOREEN TERESA*

© Copyright: Doreen Anwar, 1986

All rights reserved. No part of this publication may be reproduced, stored in a retrieval system, or transmitted in any form or by any means, electronic, mechanical, photocopying, recording or otherwise, without prior permission of the Copyright owner.

Illustrations by Marion Miller Moharram

Cover design by Ehsan el Ashmawy (AUC Artist)

First published Cairo, Egypt, 1986

Third printing 1988

Printed at the Press of the American University in Cairo
Dar El Kutub No. 2667/86
ISBN 977 424 144 4

Dedication

This anthology is dedicated to the memory of my daughter, Noreen Teresa, who helped in the collection of my writings, and of my husband Mohammed Anwar, without whose inspiration and help this work would not have been possible.

Contents

		Page
	Acknowledgments	9
	Preface	11
I	The Nile and the Land	
	(a) The Nile Festival	15
	(b) Thousand-year-old Cairo and Al-Azhar University	18
	(c) Alexandria: Seaside Resort of History and Romance	22
	(d) Into the Sa'eed—Upper Egypt	25
	(e) Portrait of an Egyptian Village	29
	(f) The Suez Canal: Reflections on its Re-opening	31
	(g) The Bridges of Cairo	33
	(h) Chaperoning (to Marsa Matruh) is Fun	35
	(i) Zamalek: Cairo's Island Suburb	36
II	The Seasons	
	(a) Shem-el-Neseem, Feast of Spring	41
	(b) Paona, Heart of the Summer	44
	(c) Autumn in Egypt	46
	(d) Egyptian Winter	48
III	Religious Feasts and Festivals	
	(a) Ramadan—Month of Charity and Blessings	53
	(b) Uncle Ali's Pilgrimage Party (Pilgrimage and Feast of the Sacrifice)	56
	(c) Moolid-el-Nabi, Birthday of the Prophet Mohammed	59
	(d) Two New Year's Days in Egypt (Moslem and Coptic)	61
	(e) Christmas in Egypt	63
	(f) Christmas and Moolid-el-Nabi Together	65

IV The Antiquities
    (a) Luxor and Aswan 69
    (b) Why not be an Egyptologist? 73
    (c) A Day at the Excavations 78

V   Aspects of Egypt
    (a) The Changing Status of Women 83
    (b) Women Pioneers 87
    (c) Health and Beauty in Egypt 88
    (d) The Street Vendors of Cairo 92
    (e) Buskers and Street-Vendors of Cairo and London 96
    (f) The Old Folks of Egypt 99
    (g) Tales for the Young in Arabic Literature 102
    (h) Mother's Day in Egypt 104
    (i) Our Bawab (Doorkeeper) 106

VI Food and Hospitality in Egypt
    (a) Egyptian Table Talk 111
    (b) The Fruits of Egypt 114
    (c) Season of Dates 117
    (d) The Day of the Apricot 119
    (e) Food for the Fast and Feast 120

VII Personal Reflections
    (a) Hamati—my Egyptian Mother-in-law 127
    (b) Two Ladies of Eighty 130
    (c) Teaching English on Two Sides of the Nile ... 132
    (d) My two Homes in Egypt and England 134

ACKNOWLEDGMENTS

The works in this anthology were included in the programmes of the *BBC,* London; *Radio London* and *Egyptian Radio;* the *Lady* Magazine, London; *The Egyptian Gazette,* Cairo; *Egypt Travel Magazine* and *Cairo Calling,* Egypt.

The author would like to express her gratitude to novelist Dr. Leslie Croxford, Director of the Freshman Writing Program at the American University in Cairo, for encouraging her to publish *Nile Reflections.* She wishes in particular to thank her colleagues and friends, Enaya Taher and Leila el Badri, for their invaluable help in reading respectively the manuscript and proofs of the anthology, Karen Boyle of the AUC Press for her painstaking proof correction, Lesley Tweddle, Managing Editor of the AUC Press, John Tyler, Publication Services Manager, Naim Atef, Art Department Manager, and Lucio Spadaccini, Printshop Manager, for their help and valuable suggestions regarding publication.

Mrs. Anwar's warmest thanks also to Laurice Kerba of the Department of English and Comparative Literature at the AUC for her ever-willing help over the years in typing the material for this book.

Notes on the Text

Translation from Arabic by Mohammed Anwar

***

Transliterations:

' Represents the Arabic letter *hamza*, which is a glottal stop. It is sometimes used in colloquial Egyptian Arabic to replace the guttural letter *qaf*, as in *'eshta (qeshta)* meaning "cream."
' Represents the Arabic velar letter *'ain*, as in *'abd*, meaning "bondsman."

***

Pharaonic illustrations:

  Frontispiece: Thebes Silver Reflector
  Endpiece of "The Antiquities": Embalmers' Mask of Anubis
  Endpiece of book: Ankh: Key of Life

Preface

This anthology of essays, broadcasts, magazine and newspaper articles has been produced over the past forty years, since I first came to Egypt with my Egyptian husband, shortly after the end of the Second World War. In Britain, I worked in the BBC Talks Department and Monitoring Service, where I met my husband.

When I came to Egypt, I worked for some years in Egyptian Radio in Cairo as Talks and Features writer and producer. Here, I had the opportunity of meeting and working with a large number of Egyptian scholars in the fields of Arabic and English literature, Egyptology, Islamic and Coptic history and culture, as my job was to edit the writings of these scholars and make them suitable for broadcasting rather than the written word to which scholars are accustomed. It was from these specialists that I gained my first interest in and insights into Egyptology, Islamic history and Arabic literature, which have been an invaluable help in my writings about Egypt. All this knowledge was later reinforced when I studied these subjects at the American University in Cairo, where I have worked for twenty-five years as a teacher of English language and research paper writing in the English Language Institute and Freshman Writing Program.

Apart from these academic studies, I had a unique opportunity of getting to understand the Egyptian way of life when I lived with my husband's family for my first fifteen years in Cairo. In particular, it was the vast knowledge of my husband and my mother-in-law of Egyptian folk lore and customs which enabled me to write with authenticity, not as an exoticist, but as one of the Egyptian community itself.

Naturally, many changes have taken place in the Egyptian scene during my forty years here, which saw Egypt change from a monarchy into a republic, to become an industrial society as well as an agricultural one, and to reap the benefits of our technological age. These changes may be inferred from the various articles and broadcasts, all of which are date-lined. For simplification, each section in the anthology has its own introduction, drawing attention to changes that have taken place in the particular area and the reason for these changes. The reader will notice that the High Dam at Aswan is often given as a reason for change in the Egyptian lifestyle. By a process of deduction, it can be seen that this dam produces quantities of cheap electricity, which in turn provide Egyptian villages with lighting, heating and television, thus making a new life for the country folk. This new way of life goes hand-in-hand with the free education for all which Egypt has enjoyed since the early part of this century.

The anthology is not intended to be a guide book or a sociological study, but it may serve as an introduction for visitors to the Egyptian scene, where I have met and worked with people of all ages and all walks of life. I personally have found Egyptians to be a happy, hospitable and generous people, laughing away their troubles with the wit and wisdom of their ages-old civilization. Some of their wisdom is evident in the sayings illustrating my articles, and to cast further light on the Egyptian ethos I have included a number of their sayings at the end of items in the anthology. (Their placing is, however, quite arbitrary, bearing no relation to the preceding text.)

The various articles and broadcasts have naturally been attuned to their respective readers and audiences, and in them I have shown what I have found in Egypt and, in my more personal reflections, expressed what I have felt about my adopted home and its people.

THE NILE
AND
THE LAND

Introduction

The main change that has come about during the period of the writing of these articles and broadcasts is that resulting from the harnessing of the Nile by the High Dam at Aswan, so that the annual flood, known since time immemorial, no longer exists. The industrialization of Egypt and the general development of the Arab world have also created great changes in the Egyptian scene. In the countryside, mechanization is gradually taking the place of methods used since Pharaonic times, replacing, for example, the buffalo-driven water wheel by the electric pump to raise water from a lower level to a higher one. Moreover, the enormous development in the now oil-rich Arab states has drawn millions of Egyptians, many of them peasants, away from the land to work in those Arab countries. Thus, life in the Egyptian countryside, which some three decades ago seemed likely to keep its age-old pattern, has changed almost out of recognition, speeded up, too, by the advent of electricity and television. Other aspects of Egypt have naturally also been affected in the course of industrialization and development, as with Cairo itself, Alexandria and the big towns. In particular, the vast population growth in the past four decades, from nineteen million to forty-six million, is a factor of vital importance in evaluating the present scene.

***

The Nile Festival

The Egyptians have, since the dawn of history, realized their complete dependence on the Nile. Their great river, which brings fertility to their almost rainless land, was even deified in ancient times. The Nile god was Hapi, and his wife the goddess Rebati, to both of whom prayers were offered that the river would continue to flow and bring its waters and rich silt to Egypt. The pharaoh Akhenaton expressed his gratitude for the river in his hymn to the one god Aton, saying that other people in the world had rain, but Aton had given the Nile to the people of Egypt for their sustenance.

The Ancient Egyptians did not know whence their river came, and while they raised their hands in gratitude for the gift of the Nile, visitors from other lands also marvelled at this unique river. In his *History,* Herodotus wondered why the Nile, at the beginning of the summer solstice, began to rise and increase for a hundred days, and then retired, continuing low throughout the winter. Later, in the 7th century A.D., The Nile amazed the Arab general 'Amr, who wrote to the Caliph 'Omar, describing the river:

> The hour comes when the river swells and roars. The waters quit their bed and flood the plains. After the river has reached its peak it subsides again and returns to its original course, leaving in its wake deposits of fertile silt. Then the people come out to plough the land and sow the seeds, and pray for abundance from their crops. (Translated by Mohammed Anwar and Doreen Anwar from Hussein Heykal's book *Al Farouk 'Omar*)

It was observed that the Nile began to rise on the eleventh day of the month of Paona (June), which was known as the "Night of the

Tear," when the goddess Isis was believed to weep for her slain husband Osiris. From that day, the river continued to rise until, in the month of Misra (August), it reached its height. These months, incidentally, are from the Coptic calendar, which in turn derived from the Ancient Egyptian solar calendar and on which the agricultural round is still based.

The Ancient Egyptians always prayed for a high flood of the Nile: they prayed for 16 ells or cubits, and the flood waters were measured accurately from the First Dynasty by means of Nileometers, one of which may be seen on the island of Rodah in Cairo. When the Nile reached its highest point on the Nileometer, a document was signed that the river had "kept its promise," and that "since the river by its beneficial flow had ensured the people's well-being, the payment of taxes had fallen due."

There was always anxiety, of course, that the river would not flood and bring its annual blessing for the fields. On the rocks at the Cataracts just beyond Aswan, an inscription tells of a famine at the time of Zoser, builder of the Step Pyramid, some 5,000 years ago. Apparently, the pharaoh wrote to the Governor of the South, expressing his deep concern:

> This is to inform you of the sorrow which has afflicted me upon my great throne . . . for the Nile has not risen for seven years . . . There is no food of any kind . . . and when the granaries are opened, nothing but air issues from them.

It was natural that the Egyptians should celebrate the annual event of the Nile flood and in fact, two festivals were held in ancient times—one in Paona on The Night of the Tear when the flood started, and again in Misra when the flood reached its height. In this month, it is said, "all the dried-up streams flow." Over the centuries, these festivals have been celebrated in different ways, and many legends sprang up around the Nile and its festivals. One of these—the most persistent—was that of the "Bride of the Nile," which said that a maiden was sacrificed each year to the Nile god. This legend, though perhaps stimulating to the imagination, has in fact no foundation, and Egyptologists affirm that there is no record of any such sacrifice having taken place. In her profound study, *The*

Nile in Egyptian Literature, Dr. Ne'maat Ahmed Fouad wonders whether the legend was invented by the Arabs, or whether it already existed when they came. According to Egyptologists, the story of the Bride of the Nile may have been spread by the Greek historian Plutarch, and later quoted by other Greek and Roman writers. The late Egyptologist, Dr. Selim Hassan, quoted by Dr. Ne'maat Ahmed Fouad, said the legend is nowhere mentioned in Egyptian writings, but in the Harris Papyrus dating from Ramses III (1198-1168 B.C.) mention is made of shrines to the Nile god along the river, at each one of which a priest collected offerings to Hapi. Wreaths of flowers in the shrines were renewed each day, and each shrine had statues in sycamore wood of Hapi and his goddess-wife Rebati. At the Festival of Hapi at the beginning of the summer solstice, these statues were cast into the river and new ones erected in the sanctuaries. It may well be that this ceremony gave rise to the legend of the Bride of the Nile.

Nowadays, since the building of the dams at Aswan, the same anxiety no longer exists that the river will not flood sufficiently and that, in consequence, the land will not be irrigated and the granaries will be empty. But the awareness of the people of Egypt of their dependence on the river and their love for it remain a part of their cultural inheritance.

Cairo Today, August 1981

***

*Close the door from which the wind comes
and be comfortable.*

Thousand-Year-Old Cairo and Al Azhar

Cairo is said to be one of the most thrilling places in the world to approach by air, when the green valley suddenly appears from out of the waste of desert, or at night, with all its myriads of twinkling lights, and the Nile winding gracefully around the city. One of the most remarkable aspects of Cairo from the air is probably the visible contrast between the ancient and modern—the old city of the Fatimids and Saladin and, side by side with it, the splendid modern capital with its towering buildings, wide squares and network of overpasses.

But by whatever means Cairo is approached, the visitor is struck by its unique panorama, where old and new exist so harmoniously together. From the eastern side of the Nile, where on the high Mokattam hills the Citadel stands sentinel over the city, the whole of thousand-year-old Cairo stretches out, with its mosques and minarets, its sky-scrapers and tree-lined avenues, over the Nile bridges to Gezira with its clubs and gardens, and on to where, at the beginning of the desert plateau, stand the relics of Egypt's most ancient past—the Pyramids of Giza.

The modern town of Cairo was founded by the Fatimids a thousand years ago, though its history may be traced back beyond this to Ancient Egyptian and Greco-Roman times. City of 1,000 minarets and over 10 million inhabitants, it is today characterized by modern architecture and buildings, world famous hotels, immense department stores, luxurious restaurants, and in the suburbs, wide gracious boulevards and avenues. It is a commercial hive of banks and shops, a kaleidoscope of old and new, and through it runs the Nile, along which spring gardens and parks, luxury hotels and casinos—a world of colour and sunshine, entertainment and life.

"I entered into the Metropolis of the Universe, into the garden of the world," the Arab historian Ibn Khaldoun wrote of Cairo in the 14th century, while in the same century, the renowned Arab traveller, Ibn Battuta, described Cairo as "mother of cities, . . . mistress of broad regions and fruitful lands, boundless in multitude of buildings, peerless in beauty and splendour." Every visitor must wish to express sentiments similar to these when he sees Egypt's capital, a city of the present and the past.

A few years ago, Cairo celebrated its millennium, marking the date of its founding by a Fatimid army which came from Qairawan in North Africa in August 969 A.D. and entered Egypt unopposed. The commander was called Johar, a Sicilian of Greek origin who had been converted to Islam. He settled outside the former capital of Al Fustat and marked out nearby the foundations of the new city. He called it Al Qahira, the Victorious, now known as Cairo. The Fatimid Dynasty also established the University of Al Azhar, the oldest existing university in the world.

The year 969 A.D. is by no means the beginning of the story of Cairo. There was a capital city in more or less this place in earliest times. The site, at the head of the Nile Delta, is an obvious one. The Ancient Egyptians of the Old Kingdom had their capital at Memphis, or Saqqara as it is known today, only a few miles from present-day Cairo. The desert plateau where they built the pyramids is the necropolis of that capital, which was established when Upper and Lower Egypt were united for the first time about 5,500 years ago.

In the Middle Kingdom and New Kingdom the capital was at Thebes in Upper Egypt, until the Pharaoh Akhenaton, the first to believe in the idea of one god only—he worshipped the power behind the sun—made his capital at Tel-el-Amarna further down the river. His capital was, however, destroyed when the Amun-Ra cult was re-established. Much later, when Alexander the Great came to Egypt, he gave his name to a new capital at the mouth of the Delta, and Alexandria remained the chief city during Greco-Roman times.

It was not until the coming of the Arabs in the 7th Century A.D. that the capital returned to its ancient site at the head of the Delta, when 'Amr ibn al 'As, the commander of the Arab forces established his camp in the place now known as Old Cairo just a few miles upstream from the present city. He called it "Al Fustat," meaning "The Camp," and during recent years there have been many excavations at this site of the first Arab settlement in Egypt. 'Amr was very impressed when he first saw Egypt—as well he might be, after the desert lands he had come from. He wrote to his caliph at Medina, describing the River Nile at this point, and how it flooded and made the land fertile: "There is a river, 0 Commander of the Faithful, blessed in its coming and going," he said. With his army, he settled beside it and built a mosque there for the worshippers of the new faith. This first mosque in Egypt, the mosque of 'Amr, with its curious, curved minaret, is a familiar landmark today.

One might well ask why, with such a perfect position for a capital, the Fatimids should find it necessary to move it. The trouble was that it was a little too close to the Nile. In those far-off days the annual flood was often disastrous, so a new site was planned on higher ground away from the danger. This new city of Cairo was surrounded by walls, like all cities of that time, and fragments of them still exist, as well as some of the old city gates. Since then Cairo has continued to grow in size and population. Great new buildings and fine hotels line the river bank, and on the outskirts to the north and south of the city there are factories of all kinds, including cotton weaving, car manufacture, cement, iron and steel works, fruit canning and plastics.

Thousand-year-old Cairo is indeed a fantastic city, and Al-Azhar University, which the Fatimids built a thousand years ago, is a descendant of a noble line of educational establishments in Egypt. Moreover, if Al Azhar is the oldest existing university in the world, that of Un, the City of the Sun, (called by the Greeks Heliopolis), was the world's first university ever established. Un, where Plato is reputed to have studied, was the scene of the earliest sun cult, and existed from pre-dynastic times until the time of the Greeks. The present-day university of Ein Shams ("Spring of the Sun") is named after Un, and was established after the second World War. At the time of Alexander the Great, and throughout the Ptolemaic, Hellenistic, Roman and early Christian periods, the centre of learning was at Alexandria, where it remained until the coming of the Arabs, and was known as "The Museum," or "Home of the Muses."

Many systems of education used now in the West originated in Egypt. In ancient times, the temple was the centre of learning: the Professors were the priests and scribes, and according to *The Legacy of Egypt,* Greek authors themselves say that Plato and other philosophers such as Thales, Solon, Pythagoras and Democritus of Abdera studied at the feet of these learned men. More recently, this same system was practised at Al Azhar, where a professor, first authorized by other professors, would take a chair and sit by a pillar of the mosque and the students would sit around him on the ground, (from which the idea of "chair" in universities developed).

Also, the position of "reader" in the university was taken from that of reader of the Qor'an, an official position at Al Azhar and other mosques. The institution of colleges also originated at Al Azhar, where students are accommodated according to the country they come from, while the Sheikh of the college is similar to the Provost in some English universities.

Al Azhar represents a whole system of free education throughout the country, beginning with the primary school. Before entering the Al Azhar primary school, children have to learn the Qor'an by heart in a kuttab, or school in the village mosque. (The late President Sadat attended such a kuttab.) As a result of this system, children go on to primary school, secondary school and university a little older than elsewhere. My husband, who taught Engineering at Al Azhar until a few years ago, said that he found students there more mature than those he had taught at other Egyptian universities. This he attributes to the fact that before entering Al Azhar University they study at its schools, in addition to the usual subjects taught elsewhere, a wide spectrum of religious subjects and go deeper into the study of Arabic language and literature and associated subjects.

Apparently, people have always made endowments for grants for students at Al Azhar to live and study, and in waqfs, or entails, there was nearly always something for "seekers of learning." Sometimes, these have been in the form of loaves of bread, while students, who come from all over the world, live free in colleges provided by endowments. One of the endowments in the past was, it seems, for transportation for the Sheikh of Al Azhar, in the form of a she-mule!

All this reverence for learning in Egypt in general goes back both to ancient times and to Islam. A wise man of Ancient Egypt, voyaging up the Nile with his son, told him: "Give thy heart to learning and love her like a mother, for there is nothing that is so precious as learning." In the same spirit, a saying of the Prophet Mohammed is: "Seek learning from the cradle to the grave," while another enjoins the faithful: "Seek learning, even if you have to go to China."

B.B.C. "Home This Afternoon," 1969
Cairo Today, March, 1983

*A craft in your hands is a
safeguard against poverty.*

***

Alexandria
Seaside Resort of History and Romance

August corresponds roughly to the Coptic month of Misra, celebrated until the building of the High Dam as the month of the inundation, when the Nile Festival was observed with great rejoicing. It is also the month of holidays, when school is over, and the people of Egypt take leave of the inland towns for a brief spell and make for the coast: in particular, they head northward for Alexandria, the ancient city of history and romance.

Egypt's great city of Alexandria is not only a vast Mediterranean port with an historical background of almost incomparable interest, but also a delightful seaside resort, with endless stretches of golden sands and perfect bathing beaches, with brilliant sunshine tempered always by a cool breeze blowing from the north and with facilities for every kind of sport and entertainment. From Cairo, it can be reached by several means: by air, by the desert road, by the agricultural road, or by train through the delta. The journey by the desert road can be made by car or air-conditioned bus, affording the visitor an exciting panorama of the desert-scape and the developing scene, while those by the agricultural road and railway show the everyday life of the countryside and the people who live and work there.

From the great port of Alexandria, ships sail for the various Mediterranean ports, and for Crete, Cyprus and the Greek islands. Cruises can be arranged from here, and many different lines of ferryboats ply between Alexandria and the European ports, carrying passengers and cars.

Alexandria itself, whose fascination has been recorded by modern writers such as E.M. Forster (*Alexandria: a History and a Guide*) and Laurence Durrell (*The Alexandria Quartet*) can be explored by car along the Corniche from Ras-el-Tin Palace at the Western Harbour to Montazah Palace (of ex-king Farouk), then slightly further on to Abu Qir, where the British fleet under Nelson fought that of Napoleon in 1798. A most interesting journey can be made a short distance inland by tram through different parts of the town, and from Ramleh (Sands) Station, keeping parallel with the coast.

A drive along the coast conjures up the great panorama of history that the city has known, and the figures of those immortals who have made their contribution to the story of Alexandria flash before the mind's eye: its founder Alexander the Great, and Cleopatra, last of the line of the Ptolemies; Julius Caesar, Mark Antony and the Roman legions; St. Mark, founder of the Christian Church in Egypt; Origen, famous sage of the early Christian era, and all the great Greek philosophers and writers who studied at the University of Alexandria and whose learning mingled so happily with that of Egypt to create the great Hellenistic civilization.

When Alexander the Great entered Egypt in 332 B.C. with his victorious armies and overcame the Persian rulers, he chose a small fishing village called Rakotis opposite the island of Pharos (later to be the site of the famous lighthouse). It was strategically well placed to become the great commercial and cultural centre that Alexander envisaged, and gave easy access to the other parts of his empire. This seaport, named after its founder, served for over 1,000 years as Egypt's capital and soon developed into a prosperous city. It is interesting to note that two of the main streets of ancient Alexandria—Canopian and Soma—correspond to two important streets of the present-day town, Hurreyya Street and Nebi Daniel Street, and were then, as now, centres for the commercial and political life of the capital. It is believed by some that Alexander's tomb, which is still sought, once lay at the crossing of these two streets. The little fishing village of Rakotis was in what is now known as Anfushi Bay, which lies at the western end of Alexandria's extensive coast line. This site chosen by Alexander still serves as the harbour, and travellers by sea will embark and disembark at the place where Menelaus landed on his return from Troy three thousand years ago.

Alexandria flourished for many centuries, finally coming under Roman rule after the death of Cleopatra. Place names along the coast remind one of this period—Camp Caesar and Cleopatra—while in the Greco-Roman Museum in the centre of the modern town, a great deal of the story of ancient Alexandria may be pieced together from the wonderful collection dating from the 3rd Century B.C. to the 3rd Century A.D., relating to the Hellenistic civilization in Egypt, and the Roman and early Christian periods. The catacombs of Kom-El-Shouqafa to the west of the city, with their wall-paintings and scenes from ancient mythology, also help to give a picture of life and beliefs in ancient Alexandria. Close by is the so-called "Pompey's Pillar," erected for the Emperor Diocletian around the year 297 A.D., and described by the 14th century Moroccan traveller, Ibn Battuta, as "awe-inspiring, . . . another of the marvellous things in this beautiful city."

Although the capital of Egypt moved to a site near that of present-day Cairo with the coming of the Arabs, Alexandria shows many evidences of Moslem Egypt. To the east of Anfoushi Bay stands the fort of Sultan Qait Bey, built for defense against the Ottomans in the latter part of the 15th Century, while some fine Islamic architecture can be seen in the mosques of Abul-Abbas al-Mursi, Timraz, Al-Bousiri, Sidi Gaber (now name of the railway station for the beaches) and Sidi Bishr (now name of a beach).

Alexandria attracts the visitor at any time of the year, but it is in summer that her true splendour is realized. The countless beaches that are linked by the Corniche and which have grown up with the modern town are undoubtedly the greatest attraction for the summer visitor. Here in the season the golden sands are gay with parasols, and the bathing cabins and casinos along the sea-front are filled with holiday-makers. In the blue waters of the Mediterranean—the "delicious sea" as E.M. Forster described it—one can swim and sunbathe to the heart's content, for the sun is always shining, and the waves lap invitingly upon the beaches.

And when at the end of the day the holiday-maker has finished his round of sightseeing or has come back sun-tanned and glowing from the healthy sea-breeze, another round of pleasure awaits him—the brilliant night-life of Alexandria. In the town itself and along the Corniche there are innumerable casinos, hotels and night-clubs, as well as cinemas, theatres, orchestral concerts and entertainment for every taste. Under the star-lit heavens and beside the lapping waters of the Mediterranean, the visitor can sit and watch the bobbing lights of the fishing fleet out at sea, and muse upon this famous city, and all that has gone to make it beautiful and great.

Egypt Travel Magazine, 1953
Cairo Today, August 1982

***

The carpenter's door is off its hinges

***

Into the Sa'eed—Upper Egypt

For me, visiting Upper Egypt was not merely seeing the marvels of Egypt's great civilisation of the past—the noble temples of Luxor and Karnak, the tombs, with their wonderful paintings and their atmosphere of peace and serenity, and the solemn grandeur of the western hills rising sheer behind the Valley of the Kings and Queens; it was not merely seeing the Nile in all its strength and beauty at Aswan, harnessed by the dam, but still pursuing its majestic course through the Cataracts and the many small islands dotted in its path. It was all this, and something more. It was penetrating into *Sa'eed el Goani,* or the depths of Upper Egypt, and seeing something of this other greater, more remote part of Egypt, where the people speak with a different accent and look different, too—sterner and more rugged—where the townships are far from the capital and newspapers are a day old when they reach their destination.

This other part of Egypt, with its different appearance and atmosphere, at once charmed and fascinated me. In Cairo and the Delta, one is accustomed to picking out certain features and characteristics in people as hailing from Upper Egypt. Many—if not most—of the workmen we see engaged in building blocks of flats are *Sa'eedi,* or Upper Egyptians. They are well known for their ability in this type of work, and for the choruses they sing to provide the necessary rhythm for certain tasks. Doubtless at night, gathered around their camp-fires, their stern features illuminated by the darting flames, they are speaking with nostalgia of their homes in the Sa'eed, and planning to go back there just as soon as the job in hand is done. Moreover, most of the fruit-vendors come from Upper Egypt—from Girga province in particular—and if sometimes we miss our familiar seller, with his well-known song, it is possible that he has taken a few days off to see his home and family.

One of the main differences between Upper and Lower Egypt is that of climate, and it was not long before I was made acutely aware of this difference. I had been warned of the bitter cold of the night and early morning, but I was not prepared for this sharp, dry cold that strikes like a knife. For the long train journey we had brought overcoats and blankets, but they were barely sufficient. In the chill light of dawn, when we had our first glimpse of the Sa'eed, we discovered that we had unconsciously adopted the head-dress of the *Sa'eedi*—a woollen beret or cap, with a thick woollen scarf wound over the head and ears and thrown over the shoulders. And the farmer from Upper Egypt does not only protect himself from the bitter cold of this region, but he sees to it that his animals are protected too. Buffaloes, cows and even our old friend the donkey—sturdy though he is known to be—all are provided with overcoats of sacking, which the farmer leaves on them until well into the day, when the sun is high and powerful in the sky.

Here in Upper Egypt, as in all country districts, everybody talks agriculture. Even in the train, it is not long before one is discussing with one's fellow travellers the success of this or that crop, or the suitability of the soil and climate of this part of the country for the growing of certain vegetables. And so it was not long before I knew that Esna was famous for its lentils, Edfu for *fool akhdar*, or broad beans, Manfalote for pomegranates, Assiut for crab-apples, and a certain kind of dates and Komombo for its sugar-cane. Something of the processes connected with the sugar industry were explained to me as the train made its way through the fields: how this land, thirty or so years ago, was desert, and had been rendered fertile by pumping the Nile water up to the higher level by machinery; how the sugar cane is planted and cultivated for three successive years, then the land ploughed and re-sown with other crops; how the outside skin is stripped off the plant and left on the land to act as a sort of manure, and to destroy pests. On the return journey, after I had drunk deep at the well of Pharaonic civilization, and had feasted my eyes upon some of the wonderful paintings and bas-reliefs which tell us of the every-day life of the Ancient Egyptians, I gazed out over these same fields and realized how little the scene had changed over all these thousands of years. The one big change in the scene was the appearance of the machine, and here in the fields of sugar-cane the tractor was busy ploughing the land which had

26

been turned, over the centuries, by the wooden, buffalo-drawn plough.

There are other peculiarities of Upper Egypt which make its general aspect quite different from that of the Delta. One of these we noticed at Baliana when we were on our way to Abydos, which is famous for being the burying-place of the earliest kings of Egypt, and also for being the centre in ancient times of the cult of Osiris—"First of the Westerners," "Lord of Eternity," "Judge of the Dead." Baliana is a lovely, verdant place. The land is a brilliant green in winter, and sparkling streams, reflecting the blue sky, lap pleasantly along beside the fields. Dotted everywhere on the landscape are little peasant dwellings, built from the golden stalks of plants. These, we were told, the peasants construct during the winter, when they bring their cattle to graze on the rich crop of clover which covers the fields after the Nile flood. The peasants settle in their temporary homes for about three months, making the year's supply of clarified butter from the rich yield of their cows and buffaloes.

Another thing in the Sa'eed which you have to get used to—apart from the difference in the Arabic dialect—is the bread. Every place in the world seems to have its own way of baking bread, and many people regard the change in their bread diet as one of the most attractive features of a holiday. The bread you eat in Upper Egypt is called *shamsi,* so named because of the fact that it is left in the sun to ferment before being baked. I found it delicious—but perhaps that was because I was on holiday and enjoying the change!

In the mid-session holiday, sometime about the beginning of February, Upper Egypt is alive with students from the schools and universities. It is perhaps one of the best aspects of the educational system in Egypt that offers to students the opportunity of touring their country and getting acquainted with its many different facets. Many of them manage to combine business with pleasure, visiting the antiquities and savouring the joys of a winter holiday in ideal weather, while perhaps at the same time touring engineering works and constructions which are associated with their courses of study. For students of architecture, Upper Egypt is a happy hunting-ground, and the temples and monuments with which the whole area abounds provide them with some wonderful first chapters in the history of art and architecture. While we were visiting Edfu and its beautiful temple which Ptolemy III dedicated to Horus, the hawk-headed god, and his wife Hathor, goddess of beauty and joy, we found ourselves in the midst of a party of students of architecture from Cairo University. The wonderfully preserved temple was obviously of the greatest interest to the students, as from it one can get a perfect idea of the construction of temples in Ptolemaic times and, moreover, of many of the rituals which used to be performed within its precincts. The temple of Horus consists of six courts, with the door apertures gradually widening at each court, so that the chanting of the priests in the inner sanctuaries could be heard by the people outside in the public courtyard. Our students of architecture had obviously not taken long to realize the good acoustics of the place, which they were putting to the test by chanting in solemn tone inside the holy of holies, while their comrades judged the volume of the sound in the outer courts.

Apart from the other groups of students, there was at Luxor a small party of students of Egyptology who had come to Upper Egypt to conduct a short course of study in the field. There was one American student in the group; the rest were Egyptians, and there were Egyptian professors from the universities of Cairo and Alexandria, as well as the Inspector of Antiquities for Luxor and Aswan, to provide technical information. Here, the students were able to see the work of excavation which is going on at present, and to observe the patient jobs of restoration carried out by the experts, some of whom have been engaged for decades on, perhaps, one small shrine or the study of a particular temple. Perhaps they could examine the work carried out by the architects of the Antiquities Department for the strengthening of certain monuments, and learn more of the tireless work that is going on to preserve for posterity that which has been preserved for us over the centuries.

[Added, 1970]

Students and tourists alike now penetrate even deeper into the Sa'eed, beyond Luxor and Aswan to Nubia, where the High Dam is rapidly changing the upper reaches of the Nile in Egypt into a modern industrial centre—into a boom town, some say. The Aswan Dam, built at the beginning of this century, brought new life to the people of the Valley, but at the same time has played a big part in destroying some of the antiquities, and a constant struggle is waged against the rising sub-soil waters and the dampness which the new irrigation systems have brought with them. In the same way, the High Dam has necessitated the removal of the great temple of Abu Simbel and the fascinating and unique Nubian settlements in the region. Few people can have failed to pause in reflection that so many relics of Egypt's past have been thus affected by the building of the dams, but the consolation must be that they are giving instead the means of creating a great new civilization in our own time.

Egyptian Radio, 1952.

***

Stretch your legs according to your quilt.

***

Portrait of an Egyptian Village

It is not a typical Egyptian village I am going to talk about: the little collection of flat-roofed dwellings in the middle of cultivated fields, with the minaret of a mosque peeping above the roofs and a few pigeon-cotes and palm-trees to complete the picture. The village I am speaking of now is a particular one: nestling at the foot of the desert plateau, on the sandstone road leading up to the Sphinx and three Great Pyramids, it has a character all its own. Unlike other Egyptian villages, it is not surrounded by green fields of vegetables or clover, nor by stretches of low bushes with their yellowish-white bolls of cotton. This village lies beside a canal, and behind it there are date-palm groves; but on the aspect overlooking the pyramids there are no fertile fields: only the barren, rocky desert sands and dunes stretching as far as the eye can see.

It is the position of this village that makes it different from the rest of the country. For thousands of years, the people who live here have been connected with this burial ground of the pharaohs; they have had little time for the usual occupations of the Egyptian peasant: the sowing and harvesting, and driving the livestock out each day to graze. In ancient times, there is little doubt that the ancestors of these villagers played their part in the building of the pyramids and sphinx. How could it have been otherwise when their homes were next door to the place chosen by the pharaohs for their necropolis? Or perhaps in ancient times the workers came to the area expressly to help in the building of these monuments. When the pharaohs died, the villagers must surely have watched the funeral processions from the valley temple so near to their own homes. They must have seen the priests with their shaven heads, sandalled feet and linen tunics, walking in solemn pace behind the sarcophagus of the mummified pharaoh: watched the incense bearers and the mourners, tearing their hair and wailing in the manner shown in some of the tomb paintings in the Valley of the Kings at Luxor and Saqqara. Perhaps they saw the sacred sun boat carried shoulder-high, to be buried with other possessions of the pharaoh for use in his after-life. Now, some four thousand five hundred years later, the descendants of these villagers have seen the sacred sun boat excavated from its burial place; probably some of them helped in the work of bringing it out again into the bright Egyptian sunlight. Earlier in the century the inhabitants of this village either watched or helped in the work of removing the sand from the feet of the Sphinx, revealing the valley temple that had lain engulfed below.

The lives of these village folk have inevitably always been linked with the pyramids. But if in the past the villagers were concerned with the dead—with the building of their funerary monuments and with the various customs and formalities associated with their death—nowadays they are very much concerned with the living. Their main preoccupation since the re-discovery of Egypt by Napoleon's Expedition has been with the tourist: in the nineteenth century and Edwardian times in Britain it was the aristocracy and the wealthy that came to spend the winter in the sunshine and visit the ancient relics. Today, the inhabitants of Pyramids Village are busy acting as guides to tourists of more modest means who come for a few days of their annual holiday. They have been adroit in picking up enough of the more common languages to act as dragoman, or interpreter, for the British, for Americans, with a few subtle changes of expression such as calling their donkey "Washington" instead of "London," and for Frenchmen, Germans, Scandinavians, Poles, Czechs, Russians. (They have become particularly good at Russian since the building of the High Dam was begun some fifteen years ago.) Some of the villagers hire donkeys and camels to the visitor, descending like a colourful swarm of locusts with the arrival of a coachload of tourists.

When night falls on Pyramids Village, the sounds that emerge from it are like those from any other Egyptian village: the rhythmical beat of the tabla drum, the plaintive tone of the one-stringed rababa, and perhaps the song of the minstrel, telling the sad love story of *Magnun Leila*, which is not unlike that of *Romeo and Juliet*, or the adventures of the Arab knight Abu Zeid el Hilaly. At prayer-time, the call of the muezzin will sound over the village. But again at night, there is something different about Pyramids Village: in the darkness, the village folk can look out towards the Sphinx and have a free view of the Sound and Light spectacle, telling the story of Egypt's ancient past.

B.B.C., "Woman's Hour", 1972

***

The one without ears is given ear-rings.

***

The Suez Canal
Reflections on its Re-opening

The Suez Canal is open once again. To hundreds of thousands of people all over the world, this news must have something of a magic quality about it. How many must immediately recall the stories of Somerset Maugham, where the scene is set on board an east or west-bound liner, with the passengers sitting around aimlessly on deck as their vessel steams slowly in convoy through the canal. Some of the passengers are sprawled out in deck-chairs with unopened novels on their laps, a glass of whisky and soda at their side. Couples lean on the ship's rail, gazing idly at the canal-side scene, the sand-dunes and camel caravans, the palm trees and donkeys. For Somerset Maugham's passengers, this was just one of the sights on the outward-bound or homeward-bound journey: picturesque, and a welcome break in the monotony of the sea journey. And then there was the excitement of the first contact with the East at Port Said, with the little boats bobbing up and down in the harbour, surrounding the ocean liner, with their haggling vendors insisting that the passengers buy a leather pouf, a pharaonic-design handbag, embossed with a slightly improbable head of Nefertiti, copper and bronze wall plaques, leather wallets, silver medallions with scarab motifs and the like. What a thrill to bargain and buy a few souvenirs—camel whips, Turkish Delight, a huge toy camel made of rabbit skins—all hauled up the side of the liner by rope from the little skiff clinging like a barnacle to the huge vessel. And then the fun of comparing one's gains with the hauls of other passengers—the annoyance of having paid too much, the satisfaction of having got hold of a good bargain.

My own canal memories go back a good few years—too many perhaps to record here with equanimity. At the tender age of eight I found myself travelling out to the Far East with my parents, and was fascinated by my first contact with the philosophical problem which the canal presented. We were travelling on a troop-ship to Hongkong, because my mother was a Queen's Army schoolteacher, and my eyes were rapidly opening like those of Miranda to this brave new world. When our outward-bound ship passed a similar vessel going in the opposite direction through the narrows of the canal, I heard the passengers calling out to one another across the water, "You're going the wrong way," and I remember asking my mother about the significance of this, and pondering deeply with my eight years' knowledge of life about the implications of this two-way greeting. And on my return some four years later, with my romanticism well awakened by the exotic sights and sounds of the East, there was the unforgettable visit to the Port Said bazaars, the purchase of a tarboosh and Arab costume at the world-famed Simon Artz stores, and the pungent aroma of an eastern spice market which has somehow never left my nostrils. Is it possible that at that time I had a feeling I was destined to return—that this was to be my home?

Over the years this feeling persisted, and in my schooldays in England I could see myself and the canal and the Port Said Customs House inextricably bound up—and only with my war-time marriage to an Egyptian did the fantasy become reality.

A later memory of the canal and all its associations came with one of my trips to Britain in the summer, on a liner from Port Said to Tilbury, London. This time it was with my little daughter, all starry-eyed at five years old. Her only experience with boats at that age was the feluka on which we braved the Nile at flood time to go to our club: so when she was told that she was to travel by boat to England, she must have had something like this in mind. We waited at evening by the Port Said Customs House for our ship to come through the canal. Suddenly our vessel appeared out of the darkness. It was lit up from stem to stern with myriads of coloured fairy lights: a great liner heaving out of the darkness into the wide harbour. My little daughter could only gasp in wonder at this incredible sight, with no words adequate to convey her delight and amazement at this splendid vessel that had just come in convoy through the Suez Canal.

The Egyptian Gazette, 1975

***

Water proves the diver.

***

The Bridges of Cairo

Like other big cities in the world, Cairo continues to expand, presenting new traffic problems for the authorities. One of the ways to overcome such problems has been to build overpasses and bridges, and probably one of the first things that strikes the visitor, or somebody returning to Cairo after an absence of some years, is the vast network of these constructions over the city and river. Latest to be opened is a new bridge over the Nile, named 15th May, replacing the old Zamalek Bridge and connecting Zamalek on Gezira (island) with the developing suburbs in Giza, on the western side of the Nile. In due course, this network will be continued over the island, replacing the present Boulaq Bridge (designed by M. Eifel, designer of the Eifel Tower in Paris) to link up with the main route to the railway station and eventually to Cairo airport, and it is interesting at this point to look back at the way Cairo's bridges have developed.

Early this century, there was only the bridge of Qasr-el-Nil, with its continuation over the other side of the island, available for those wishing to travel by road from Cairo to the Pyramids and Sphinx, or southwards, along the west bank to Upper Egypt. Since then, the metropolis has fanned out in every direction, making the matter of bridges across the river to the suburbs one of paramount importance.

Viewed from north to south, the first bridge to be seen is that spanning the river from the port of Rod-el-Farag to Embabah, and carrying the train to Upper Egypt. Before this bridge was built, the railway to Upper Egypt started from a station on the Giza side. Gezira, the island in the Nile, now is linked to the mainland by five bridges, the most recent before 15th May Bridge being that known as 6th October, a splendid construction named after the victorious 1973 war. Further southwards, Cairo is joined to Gezira by Qasr-el-Nil Bridge, which commands a wonderful view of the modern city, and to the western bank by Evacuation Bridge, beautiful in its setting: on one side the Exhibition grounds and on the other boating clubs and river craft of every description.

From here, the Nile widens and further south is spanned by University Bridge, between the Faculty of Medicine buildings and the other faculties of Cairo University. Last of the main Cairo bridges and the widest is Giza Bridge, which once carried trams as well as every other kind of vehicle, and which leads directly to the Pyramids. Some of these Nile bridges used to open at scheduled times in the day to allow river traffic to pass through, providing an unforgettable scene as the felukas negotiated the bridges and sailed on into the middle of the stream. Now, there are other scenes of Nile steamers and motor launches as well as sailing boats, and a constant stream of motor traffic traversing the many bridges, all reflecting much of the history of Cairo and the great change that has taken place in the development of the city.

Cairo Today, June, 1972

***

If you come between an onion and its skin, you only get its stench.

Chaperoning (to Marsa Matruh) is Fun!

It was so cold and dusty for a few days before the Big Feast that a few faint hearts called off. But the rest of us made the ten-hour journey to Marsa Matruh in high spirits. Admittedly, somebody lost the tickets, the tents did not arrive with us, and we spent a somewhat ticklish first night on the floor of the Employees Club (which the Governor of Marsa Matruh was kind enough to offer us), but after that it was plain sailing. The following day the beach and shopping centre were invaded by some fifty AUC students, all on the look-out for sunshine and the good things they could find during their five-day vacation. By evening the tents were up and a more comfortable night was spent by all—in the camp and in the tent annex of the near-by hotel.

The Club somehow managed to arrange that we did the usual tourist round, and made our own fun. The *carettas* or donkey-carts were kept busy taking us to local places of interest; there was a gusty sail over to Rommel's Cave and a rather apprehensive trek to Cleopatra's Bath with a duststorm on the horizon. There was swimming in the icy, turquoise waters of the bay, and transistor "twist" on the sands by day, and sneezing and fainting and sunstroke, eau-de-cologne and visits from a convenient doctor by night. There were barbecues and songs and tales round the campfire, and the moonlight roasting of the sheep. And then there was striking of the camp, last purchases from the vendor beside the hotel—beads and Siwan kerchiefs and baskets—and then by caretta back for the long train journey home, and the songs and the laughter and the Feast holiday crowds. Thank you, members of the Greek Cultural Club for a wonderful, unforgettable trip!

Caravan, American University in Cairo, 1964

* * *

The essence of man is forgetfulness.

Zamalek: Cairo's Island Suburb

Ever since I came to live in Egypt I have been attracted to Zamalek and wanted to live in this delightful suburb of Cairo. Situated on an island, or *gezira,* on the Nile, it lies between the town outskirts of Boulaq to the east and Giza governorate to the west. Its position thus makes it within comfortable distance of the centre of Cairo and all the new suburbs on the western side, while at the same time the Nile insulates it from the more congested areas. I wanted to live in Zamalek because of its position on the Nile and also because of its atmosphere, which in fact I was not able to attempt to analyze until I had lived here for some long time.

The name "Al Zamalek" has a fascinating origin. According to Mohammed Fahmy Abdel Latif, writing in the newspaper *Al-Akhbar,* the word "Zamalek" is the plural of *zamlak,* a Mameluke word meaning "screen"—a hut without a roof, like a bathing-hut, made of stiff material like linen. (The Mamelukes were warriors of several origins who ruled in Egypt at different times from Salah-al-Din—Saladin—through the Ottoman period, and ended with the reign of Mohammed Ali at the beginning of the 19th century.) It seems the Mamelukes used to make these round, tent-like constructions, and in them changed into the clothes which they wore for horsemanship, as they used this area as a place for training. Thus it became known as "the land of Zamalek," then shortened to "Zamalek."

You can find everything in Zamalek. There are old-world villas, modern apartment buildings, embassies, schools, mosques and churches, clubs, public gardens, streets of shops, and quiet tree-lined side-roads. Then there is the busy main street over which an overpass is being constructed and which may return Zamalek to something of its former peace.

It is perhaps this diversity which is the greatest charm of Zamalek, for it is neither new nor old, neither Oriental nor Western, but a blending of all. There are supermarkets next to pavement markets where peasant women sell salad greens and limes, boutiques sandwiched between a qaftan maker and carpet mender, a pavement book-stall in front of the popular confectioner's, Simonds, itinerant sellers of limes and bunches of mint importuning shoppers and weaving their way in and out of the streams of cars at traffic lights, while at evening in summer the vendors will offer you a bracelet of jasmine.

In Zamalek you will see a flock of sheep being driven by a couple of youths through streets full of luxury cars, a peasant riding his donkey along the main road in the shadow of the new overpass and a carriage with its decoration of brass hangings jingling with the rhythm of the horse's trot. There are street markets of baskets and slippers in Zamalek, perhaps a knife-grinder, juice shops, vendors roasting corn-on-the-cob and peanuts, and shops selling freshly-cooked breakfast dishes made of beans—the cheapest and most nourishing meals in the world. On trays on the pavement, a baker spreads his freshly-baked loaves, rolls and pastries just a stone's throw from the vast Omar Khayyam Marriott Hotel, which is itself an artistic mixture, with the new addition built around the splendid palace which Ismail Pasha constructed in 1869 to celebrate the opening of the Suez Canal.

Thursday is a great day in Zamalek. The butchers decorate their shops gaily with coloured lights for the week-end, with paper rosettes on the meat carcasses, while the flower shops perfume the air with their bouquets and flower arrangements for weddings. On Thursdays, too, there are more than a few wedding cars, festooned with rosettes, balloons and streamers, and the incense seller swings his censer among the crowds, calling a blessing on all.

Zamalek celebrates all the festivals with gusto, whether it be Ramadan, Christmas, the Feast of the Sacrifice, Birth of the Prophet Mohammed or Shem-el-Neseem. According to the feast, the minarets are illuminated, the flower shops filled with exquisite flower arrangements, their pavements decked with wreaths, bouquets, and flowering plants of all kinds. At the confectioners, you can find oriental sweetmeats for Ramadan and puddings and pies for Christmas, while fruit shops vie to display the best of fruits in season, lovingly arranged and re-arranged throughout the day.

Another reason why I love Zamalek is because the people are so friendly and welcoming. Certainly, things have changed in the twenty or so years since we first came here. The children have grown up and no longer follow their father's trade. The eldest son sometimes does, it is true, as with the upholsterer, who is carrying on his father's thriving business. But his younger brother went to the Faculty of Dentistry and is now working in Upper Egypt. The fruiterers' sons, too, are educated and entering the professions: one got very high grades and has just finished his first year in Medicine, while the son of another fruiterer is at the Faculty of Arts, studying Persian and Hebrew. Both, however, help their fathers during the long summer holiday, and when they are not studying. With the change in education and profession, though, the younger generation are wearing T-shirts and jeans, while their fathers still adhere to their traditional qaftans. Despite these changes, these young folk follow the pattern of their fathers in their friendly and welcoming manner, which is surely something inherent in the Egyptian nature.

The new overpass is designed to relieve the traffic congestion in Zamalek, taking cars from the western suburbs over Zamalek and into town on the eastern side. I wonder whether it will serve its purpose as successfully as is hoped? I cannot imagine that many but those with the most urgent business will be content to by-pass Zamalek, once a collection of Mameluke soldiers' huts, and now surely one of the most delightful areas in Egypt.

Written for *Nile Reflections*, 1985.

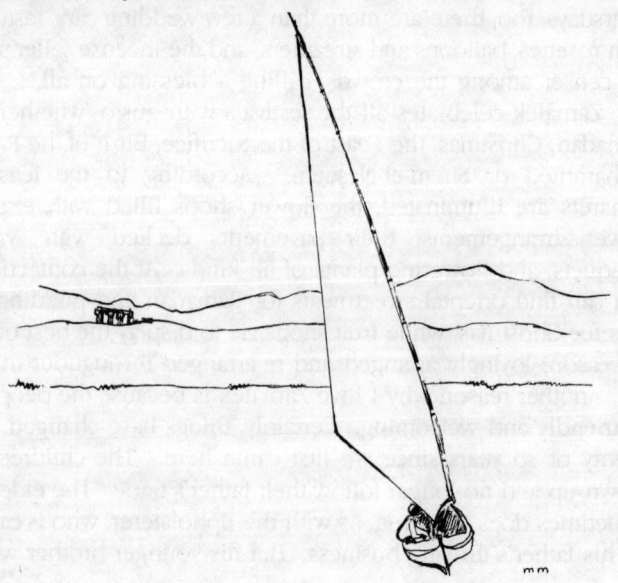

*THE
SEASONS*

Introduction

The seasons have not changed in Egypt, of course, but as a result of the building of the High Dam, sowing and harvesting no longer depend on the inundation, and there is no period when parts of the country in Upper Egypt are under flood water. This factor must be taken into consideration in articles written prior to the building of the High Dam, particularly that on autumn, which formerly was a time of luxuriant growth in Egypt, resulting from the rich silt brought down by the Nile flood. Nowadays, this growth is spread out evenly over the whole year, with resultant differentiation in rotation of crops.

Note: The various sayings connected with the months of the Coptic calendar are recorded in the Agricultural Museum in Doqqi.

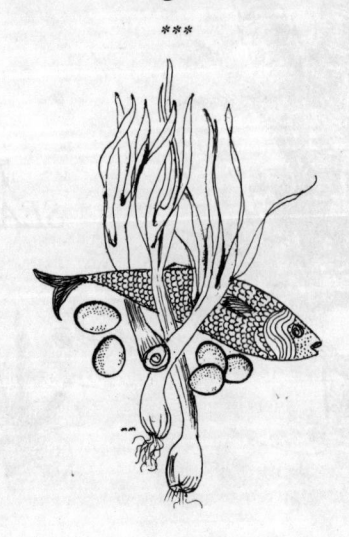

***

Shem-el-Neseem, Feast of Spring

The first sign of spring in Egypt comes one chilly February day when sprays of white apricot blossom suddenly appear in the florist's shop, sometimes surrounded by swarms of bees drinking the nectar. After a few days the blossoms disappear as suddenly as they came, and for a while the thought of spring fades from the mind. But then, little by little, more signs appear: the willow trees on the Nile banks—*saf-saaf* as they are known here—come into leaf and wave their fronds in the light breeze; in the countryside, field after field of green wheat starts to ripen, and soon the street vendor will be singing his song of praise for his wares of *malana* or split peas: "The malana has ripened, and the spinster has married." This is in late March, or early April, and from now on the pace of approaching spring quickens. Everywhere, the flowering trees break into blossom, and there is a haze of colour in the parks and gardens—purple and pink and mauve.

The celebration of the Spring Feast in Egypt comes on the Monday following Easter Sunday, according to the calendar of the Eastern Church. The festival of *Shem-el-Neseem*, or "Smelling the sweet breeze of the North," is celebrated by all the people of Egypt, irrespective of their religion. The expression itself is found in ancient hieroglyphic inscriptions relating to the Old Kingdom, and thus it seems that inhaling the breeze from the north was one of the things most desired by the Ancient Egyptians, as it is by their descendants. Egyptians must have always realized that the north wind was a healthy wind, coming as it does from the sea, cooling the parched desert and bringing respite after the heat of a summer day. And so on Shem-el-Neseem it is customary to rise early in the morning and go out into the countryside or gardens to breathe the fresh, pure air of spring.

The Egyptian Spring Feast seems to be related to that observed by the Ancient Egyptians in their celebration of the day when Osiris was believed to have risen from the dead. According to legend, Osiris was the child of the earth and sky gods, and, after his death at the hands of his brother Set, was believed to have been resurrected. Thereafter, he was known to the Ancient Egyptians as God of the Underworld, Lord of the Westerners and Judge of the Dead. As Osiris was believed to have returned from death, it was natural that he should have been identified with spring, when life returns once more to the world. In ancient times, it was the custom early in the year to make effigies of Osiris, and to sow in this earthen effigy some seeds of wheat. In time, these seeds would sprout, sending forth green shoots, symbolizing the conquest of life over death.

Whether or not the origins of the Spring Feast can be traced to ancient times, it is obvious that many of the customs and traditions associated with it are observed for reasons of health. After *Shem-el-Neseem* follow weeks of sandstorm, or *khamaseen*, so one must take all precautions necessary to protect one's health during this period. Most likely to suffer are the eyes, and so one of the customs is to paint the eyes with *kohl* on the Saturday before *Shem-el-Neseem*. Apart from adding lustre to the eyes, the substance contains many valuable ingredients, and has been used by the Egyptians for thousands of years on grounds of both health and beauty.

Also for reasons of health, it is a habit to use *ra'ra'Ayyoub,* or Job's herb, in bathing on the Wednesday before the feast. This is the herb that is alleged to have cured the prophet Job of his skin affliction and many Egyptians believe in its valuable healing properties. Another tradition closely followed by country people is for the children to bathe and put on clean clothes on the eve of *Shem-el-Neseem*. The *Shammaamah,* or "Lady Smeller," is believed to pass by at night and any child who is not clean and fresh for the feast may expect to receive due punishment.

Onions figure largely in the celebration of *Shem-el-Neseem*. Here again, the reason is surely one of health, as they are generally considered to give protection against many illnesses prevalent in hot climates. The picnic basket for *Shem-el-Neseem* would not be complete without a good helping of spring onions, and on the eve of the feast, bunches of onions are hung over the doorway and sometimes over the bed, supposedly to drive away illness and misfortune. The use of onions for health reasons seems always to have been a practice in Egypt, and some of the representations on the Theban tombs show the priests offering great bunches of onions to the dead, while sometimes we see figures of the dead—a man and his wife, perhaps—carrying bundles of onions in their hands, while at the same time wearing a necklace of onions around their necks.

Other important items in the festive fare for *Shem-el-Neseem* are *fasseekh,* or salted fish, and all kinds of green vegetables, either fresh or cooked. Lettuce and split peas are eaten with the picnic lunch, and those who stay at home will most likely cook their favourite dish of *melokheyya,* made from a finely chopped green vegetable resembling mint in appearance. They will also probably sample the season's first dish of stuffed vine leaves.

But most important of all the customs and traditions connected with Easter and *Shem-el-Neseem* is colouring the eggs. On the Saturday before the feast, "two eggs should be eaten," says an old proverb, "to protect the health of both eyes!" These are in addition to those eaten on the day of *Shem-el-Neseem* itself.

On *Shem-el-Neseem* the whole country is on holiday: in fact, it is the only day in the year when some shops close their doors. From early morning, town dwellers make their way to the countryside and open spaces to picnic and "inhale the sweet breeze from the north". They will probably be wearing their brightly coloured summer clothes for the first time this year, as tradition has it that, similar to the English country-man's warning, "Ne'er cast a clout till May be out," people should not put aside their warm winter clothing until *Shem-el-Neseem*. Perhaps here and there will be heard the gay jingle of donkey carts with their loads of singing and dancing holiday-makers, while street vendors and entertainers add their touch of colour and romance to the celebration of this joyful ancient festival.

Cairo Today, April 1981

***

If the master of the house plays the tambourine,
don't blame the members of the household for dancing.

Paona, Heart of the Summer

It was a particularly severe winter, so perhaps it is only natural that we should be having a rather trying summer this year in Egypt. I was getting into the lift the other day, gasping with the heat and fanning myself with my newspaper. "My word, it's hot," I complained to the lift attendant, in my best Arabic. If he was feeling the heat, the attendant certainly concealed the fact admirably. But he agreed with me that it was hot and, shrugging his shoulders and lifting his eyebrows, he asked me how after all, we could expect it to be otherwise. "It's Paona," he said.

Paona is the tenth month of the Coptic calendar, which is relied on to a great extent for the agricultural round in Egypt. It corresponds roughly to June of the western calendar, and this month is regarded as the height of summer. The country people say: "The heart of the summer is Paona; the heart of the winter is Tooba." They also say that "Paona splits the stone," meaning that the heat is intense at this time.

The Egyptian summer is considered by agriculturalists to consist of the months of Bashans, Paona and Abib, corresponding roughly to the period from mid-May to mid-August. The following month, Misra, is the month of the inundation, and by then, therefore, summer is regarded as practically over. During these three months of summer, the wheat harvest is gathered and stored. Of Bashans, it is said: "It sweeps the fields clean," and the peasants are busy during this month winnowing and threshing the wheat. In Paona, the grain is stored. This is also the main time for sheep shearing, and the time for the ripening of gemaize, the fruit of the sycamore tree. It is, in fact, just now that this marvellous tree is in full leaf in Egypt, affording its welcome shade to the peasants and to their farm animals in the heat of the day. The sycamore tree is a typical feature of the Egyptian countryside, and there is probably no village without one. It is under its spreading branches that the country folk rest at noon, and gather to talk over the day's happenings when evening comes. Beneath it too, no doubt, many of the village dramas are enacted, and those who saw the Arabic film *Zeinab* will remember that it was under the sycamore tree that the lovers met, both in the time of their happiness and of their sorrow. Indeed, the sycamore plays such a big part in the life of the country people, that it is not at all surprising to learn that it was regarded as sacred in ancient times, associated with the sky goddess Nut, mother of the gods.

There are great contrasts in temperatures in the land of Egypt, and while the coastal towns enjoy moderate temperatures, Upper Egypt is sweltering at 40 degrees in the shade! Notwithstanding this, there is a part of Egypt, far away in the deep south, that lives only in the summer. Beyond Aswan, the beautiful island of Philae rises out of the waters at this time, and for a brief spell we can see the Temple of Isis, which for the rest of the year lies submerged and only comes to light when the sluice gates of the Aswan Dam are opened to the full. For these summer months we can see Philae and guess at its ancient glory, but then again comes the inundation, and Philae is gone with the passing of summer.

In Cairo, the summer scene is a brilliant one—blue sky, green Nile, white sails of the river craft, and the silvery flash of the herons over the river at sunset. But most brilliant of all is the red of the flamboyant trees and the green of their leaves. Beneath our feet is a carpet of red blossoms, and a lizard scuttling through the scorched leaves; above our heads a canopy of red, and the busy twitter of nesting birds. At night, a silver moon is reflected in the unruffled surface of the river and there is the scent of jasmine in the air.

But with the coming of summer, our thoughts go northwards. During recent years, Egypt has become conscious of her delightful seaside resorts—Alexandria, Marsa Matruh, Abu Qir, Ras-el-Bar, Baltime—and gradually the coastline is opening up for summer holidays. For the call of the sea is irresistible, and our minds are full of the Mediterranean and the sound of the sea is in our ears when summer comes.

The Egyptian Gazette, June, 1953

***

*The hell of a relation
is better than the paradise of a stranger.*

Autumn in Egypt

The long, low shadows slant across the fields and remind us that autumn has come. "Autumn!" some may exclaim, with a start of surprise, when they remember what the season means to them in their northern lands across the sea. They will remember the leaves "yellow, and black, and pale, and hectic red," so soon to be driven from the trees by the west wind: they will recall the first sharp morning frosts and the sense of exhilaration they bring, and the birds—those fickle companions of spring and summer now on the wing to warmer climes; they will think of the strange mixed feelings "sweet though in sadness" with which they regard the dying year. "Autumn roses, mournful roses" is how Chekov described the bouquet brought in from the misty garden at the end of the year, heralding the time when the land would be silent and sleeping, waiting for the quickening of spring.

This, indeed, is not the autumn of Egypt. Here there is no wild west wind to scatter the leaves and, in fact, many of the trees are evergreen. There are no frosts; flowers are more profuse than ever. Even the self-same birds that so recently left their northern homes are now making their appearance in this country. No, autumn has an entirely different significance in Egypt. The message it brings is not of the dying year: on the contrary, it is at this time that the Nile has deposited its fertile silt on the land, and the Egyptian sees in its present glorious colour of chocolate and blue a promise of the time soon to come when the valley will burst into green, filled with the crops of winter.

Autumn is here, however, as in other countries, a season of "mellow fruitfulness." The date-palms are heavy now with their golden clusters, and other trees bear their strange, mature fruits that ripen after summer. And later, when the autumn fruits are over, the citrus fruits of winter—having "drunk of the Nile waters," as the Egyptians put it—will begin to swell and ripen.

The Coptic month of Toot, the beginning of autumn, is known as *Rotab Toot*, or the month when dates become ripe and tender. This is also the time of the cotton harvest, and when the cotton has been gathered there will be scenes of rejoicing throughout the countryside. During its long period of growth, the peasant has tended the crop carefully, for he knows that his livelihood depends upon it. As he weeded between the rows of cotton bushes, searching for any signs of pests, he would make his plans for the time when the crop was harvested and sold. And when the picking season came, he would discuss with his fellow workers in the cotton fields his plans for spending his profits.

While the men were talking of buying a few more feddans to add to their holdings, the women would be gossiping away about the marriages that would take place in the village when the harvest was home. And so autumn is a season of weddings and festivity in the Egyptian countryside, for the peasants have money in their pockets and they can relax for a while and enjoy the fruits of their labour.

But the peasant cannot pause for long, as now begins his busiest time on the land. In the summer, there is little apart from the cotton and maize crops, but now that the Nile has brought its fertilizing silt, the peasant must begin to prepare the ground for the abundant crops of winter. Foremost among these is *berseem,* or clover, which is grown as fodder for the animals, and calving time is so arranged as to coincide with this crop, in order that the mothers may yield rich milk. The buffalo—Egypt's chief milk-producing animal—is not very beautiful, but her milk is twice as rich as that of the cow and her ungainliness is compensated for by a corresponding amount of strength, rendering her much less susceptible to tuberculosis.

When the month of Toot is over, next comes Baba, the second month of the Coptic year. At this time, the country people say: "Go in and shut the door," which can be taken to mean either that there is money in the house after the cotton harvest, and so one should beware of thieves, or that winter is coming and the days of sitting in the warm sunshine before the open door are over. It is quite likely that the saying implies both these meanings.

The last month of autumn is known as Hatoor, which name is derived from Hathor, the Ancient Egyptian goddess of love and joy. This is the most important time for sowing, and the peasants say: "If you miss sowing during Hatoor, then you will have to wait until next year." Wheat, barley, beans, flax, onions, and lentils are among the crops sown then and Hatoor is known as "the month of the sowing of the golden seed."

Autumn in Egypt is indeed a golden time, and it is doubly blessed. It is a time of ripening and fulfilment, and at the same time of beginning anew. The land has yielded its riches, the Nile has brought its great gift of fertile soil, and the Egyptian peasant once again turns over the earth and plants the seed.

The Egyptian Gazette, September, 1953

***

Only the worst cows are left in the manger.

***

Egyptian Winter

"It's wintering outside," said the office cleaner, looking dejectedly at the rain pattering against the window and sending pedestrians in the street below scuttling for shelter. "Rain" and "winter" are almost synonymous in colloquial Egyptian Arabic, and the average Egyptian views the coming of the season with disgust. Perhaps for the visitor, Egypt is a winter paradise, with fog and snow unknown, with temperatures almost never dropping below freezing point, apart from a degree or two in Upper Egypt at night, and with a generous supply of sunshine for a great deal of the time. But for many Egyptians, winter signifies a period of misery, when colds are the order of the day and when, in spite of everything written in geography books, it definitely does rain.

The seasons are reckoned in Egypt by the Coptic calendar, which undoubtedly dates back beyond the Christian era into earliest times in the history of the Nile Valley, and the farmers depend on it for the agricultural round—for the sowing, reaping, and harvesting. Winter, according to this calendar, starts in the month of Kiak, which roughly corresponds to December of the Western calendar, and it is at this time that the peasant begins to wrap himself up warmly in his thick woollen scarf, and collect his firewood for the winter. He has plenty of leisure time now, for the cotton and date harvests are over and the autumn sowing completed. So he occupies himself with preparations for the cold days ahead, gathering the stalks of the cotton bushes and the brittle pods of the flame trees as firewood for the ovens, plaiting palm leaves into baskets indoors, and perhaps playing *seaga*—a game something like draughts—on the ground outdoors in the sun.

The country folk driving into market now begin to bring winter produce: huge, chill-looking cabbages, splendid white cauliflowers, leeks and carrots. Of Kiak, the peasants say: "Your morning, your evening,"—in other words, the day is over almost before it has begun. And after Kiak comes Tooba, which starts on the 9th of January, and now Egypt shivers in the depths of her winter. "Tooba," it is said, "makes the old woman shrivel up with cold," and now everywhere throughout the countryside the fires are lit, and the people gather round for the warmth and comfort they give. In the villages there are fires in the homesteads and in the fields, while in the towns the house-builders from Upper Egypt warm themselves before their camp-fires, dreaming perhaps of their homes and families as they gaze into the dancing flames.

And still, despite the cold that it brings, and sometimes the rain, the Egyptian winter has its charms. The desert becomes an inviting playground for all to enjoy; there are friendly fires burning everywhere at night; there is the inviting sight and smell of roasted corn-on-the-cob; there is fresh sugar-cane to be chewed and nourishing beverages to be consumed, such as *sahlab*, (a thick drink topped with cinnamon and chopped nuts) or *beleela*, (a gruel made of wheat or maize and served with sultanas and grated coconut). And though the cold may strike deeply and the wind blow chill, the Egyptian can always compare his lot favourably with elsewhere and reflect, as did the milkman today, that this is nothing to what they're having abroad: 50 degrees below freezing! "We're fine here," he said.

The Egyptian Gazette, January, 1979

RELIGIOUS
FEASTS AND
FESTIVALS

Introduction

Due to the mixed nature of her religious heritage, Egypt observes a number of festivals throughout the year. Though the times of these festivals have obviously not changed over the years, the way in which they are celebrated differs to some extent from the past as a result of developing technology and other factors which have influenced the Egyptian life style. A big change that has taken place over the years in which these essays were written results from the building of the High Dam in Aswan in Upper Egypt, and the ready availability of electricity throughout the countryside, as well as in the towns. Among other things, this has enabled the people to have access to television. Nowadays, therefore, instead of depending on the local bard, itinerant musicians and performers, the village folk can switch on and see it all on TV. In fact, most of these entertainers have disappeared from the streets and found their way into musical shows and TV. Aware of the disappearance of these folk entertainments, some hotels in Egypt are now building sets and recreating the scene. The reader should be aware of this changed situation when reading essays dating from some years back, before Egypt embarked on the High Dam venture.

***

Ramadan
Month of Charity and Blessings

Ramadan is with us once again: Ramadan, the Moslem month of fasting—month of charity and blessings. *Ramadan Kareem*!

The beginning of the holy month of Ramadan is proclaimed when the new crescent moon is viewed immediately after sunset. The ceremony of the *Ro'ya*, or "Observation," always takes place on the 29th day of Sha'ban, the month preceding Ramadan, and shortly before sunset, senior Moslem judges assemble at the Moslem High Court. Here they await the evidence of witnesses—there must be at least two—that the new crescent has been sighted after sunset and, should this be the case, a document is signed at the Court, announcing the beginning of the month of fasting.

Immediately the proclamation is made, seasonal greetings are exchanged: in the street outside the Court a band strikes up, and a representative of the Governor of the city, mounted on horseback, heads a procession back through the streets of the town. Until not so long ago, this used to be very picturesque, perhaps not so much unlike London's Lord Mayor's Show. Representatives of the different trades and guilds paraded, each performing on his float a scene typical of his particular trade. Here was a baker, seated before his smoking oven; here was a cook, stirring some mixture in a huge copper utensil; here a carpenter planing a piece of wood.

The news of the beginning of Ramadan is speedily conveyed to the appropriate quarters and soon minarets throughout the country are encircled by twinkling lights. In Moslem households, members of the family lose no time in wishing each other the compliments of the season, while the children, who have been anxiously awaiting the signal, light up their Ramadan lanterns and, swinging them, march through the streets chanting their traditional songs.

Ramadan was chosen as the month of fasting because it was at this time that the first revelations came to the Prophet Mohammed: to be exact, on the 27th of Ramadan, the preceding evening being known as *Leilet el Qadr* or "Night of Power." Fasting, the main feature of Ramadan, is one of the five "corner-stones" of Islam, and it is probably very surprising for the visitor to a Moslem country to discover that the great majority of people do, in fact, religiously observe the fast, and are genuinely ashamed or disappointed if, for health or other reasons, they are prevented from fasting. Indeed, the fast is regarded by many, not as a penance, but as a privilege, and children, who can understand but little of the religious significance of the fast, will plead to be allowed to partake of this privilege. For them, it is fun to get up in the small hours of the morning and eat *sohoor* with the grown-ups, and this little meal, taken shortly before dawn to sustain the faster throughout the long day until sunset, becomes in time one of the most delightful memories of childhood.

Who, indeed, could stay asleep in bed when there were so many exciting things happening? An hour or so before dawn, there is heard the rhythmic beating of a *tablah* or drum, and down the street comes the *masahharati*, awakening the fasters by name for their *sohoor*. In the early weeks of the month, his song praises God and extols the virtues of fasting:

"Ye worshippers of God,
Profess the Unity of God;
He, the ever-present and ever-vigilant.
This is the time for wishing,
And asking forgiveness from God,
Awaken, O faster,
And remember the Eternal!"

Towards the end of the month, the song of the *masahharati* is valedictory, expressing all the tenderness and affection felt at parting with a beloved friend:

"We shall miss you, month of charity and blessings,
We shall miss you, month of fasting!"

There is something particularly poignant about the *masahharati*, and his drum, and his song. Perhaps it is that his voice sets on foot a train of recollections—memories of other Ramadans long since past, of early years of fasting, of friendships made and renewed in this happiest of months.

After *sohoor*—which generally consists of light foods such as yoghourt, a special kind of beans, fruit and thirst-quenching drinks—many people go back to bed. Some wait to perform the dawn prayer, while others gather in the mosques to pray and recite verses from the Qor'an.

From dawn to sunset is the time laid down for fasting. "Dawn" is carefully defined as the time when the black thread may be distinguished from the white, and perhaps this is symbolical for the time when the first faint glimmer of light on the eastern horizon dispels the blackness of night. A gun is fired from the Citadel shortly before dawn so that fasters may prepare themselves once more.

The day wears on and, as the sunset hour approaches, a strange silence hovers like a cloud over the town. Buses and trams, usually bulging with humanity, empty as if by an unspoken command. People stand on their balconies and at windows watching the sun as it descends—almost unwillingly, it seems—a flaming ball behind the palms and dun-coloured hills. The Qor'an chanting on the radio ends; there is a minute or so of silence, and then the gun fired from the Citadel announces the end of fasting for the day.

"*Allahu Akbar, Allahu Akbar.*" "God is greater than all." Comes the call of the *mu'azzin* to the sunset prayer; "There is no god but God." The sheikh and the holy man are at prayer, but the peasant and townsman, alike exhausted by work and privation, are breaking their fast in relief and thankfulness.

For a while, a complete hush reigns over the city as the fasters take their sunset meal. The silence in the streets does not last for long, however, and soon there comes the sound of youthful voices, and there are swinging lanterns in the darkness as the children gather together to sing the songs of Ramadan.

In some households, there are lanterns hanging over the doorways, and inside can be heard the chanting of the Qor'an, and perhaps a glimpse may be caught of a room full of guests, making their Ramadan calls, listening to the chanting, and eating the nuts and sweetmeats which are offered during this month.

In some of the older coffee-houses there are recitals from the Arab romances. The minstrel tells of the adventures of the warrior-poet 'Antar, and of his love for 'Abla. He tells, too, of the exploits of Abu Zeid El Hilaly and of other poets and knights and their deeds of chivalry. The minstrel is accompanied on the *rababa*—a small stringed instrument played like the cello.

Ramadan is here, with all its traditions, customs, and memories. It is a happy month, with the spirit of good-will and generosity abounding everywhere and, with its many different aspects, standing out in sharp relief from the rest of the year. The sunset breakfast, the evenings of pleasant companionship, the songs and the chanting, the lanterns and the lighted minarets, all this makes of Ramadan a happy and well-loved month.

Egyptian Radio, May, 1948

***

The one who doesn't know how to dance says the ground is uneven.

***

Uncle 'Ali's Pilgrimage Party
(Pilgrimage & Feast of the Sacrifice)

There we were—all gathered together in Uncle 'Ali's beautiful flat overlooking the Nile in Cairo. There must have been at least fifty of us, probably more. Some of the men were sitting on the circular balcony, watching the river-craft. There was a boat-race that day, I remember, and one of the boats capsized, providing a touch of unexpected excitement. The ladies were for the most part seated inside in the large reception rooms, gossiping and talking about the children's prowess at school. Many of us hadn't seen each other for years: it's amazing that people living in the same town manage to meet so seldom. There's no doubt that social patterns are changing a lot in Egypt, but family ties are still fairly strong, and there are some occasions which bring all the members together. This was one of those occasions, because Uncle 'Ali had just returned after making the Pilgrimage to Mecca.

Performing the Pilgrimage to Mecca is one of the sacred duties of every Moslem, and there's no prouder person than the one who has made it. No wonder that Uncle 'Ali's face wore a serene expression that day, for at the age of 75 he had accomplished this duty. In future, he was entitled to be known as *El Haj,* or "The Pilgrim."

Making the Pilgrimage is of course much easier nowadays than it was in the past. Perhaps there are more formalities in the way of passports, currency, and the various inoculations and quarantine regulations. But having dealt with these, it can be just a matter of boarding a plane, and then checking in at the hotel on arrival: quite a different affair from the past, when the land journey had to be made on horse-back or by camel, or sometimes on foot, taking several weeks instead of a few hours as it does today. It was certainly much less comfortable, but perhaps it was a more companionable affair in the old days. Surely the journey was made cheerful by the pilgrims telling one another tales of their different countries, and perhaps singing to the rhythm of the camel's swinging stride. Some of the songs of those days are still preserved:

> How fortunate is he who is going! People of every race
> are going! The Egyptian, the Syrian, the Indian, the
> Chinese, the Moroccan, the Turk and the
> Sudanese—they are all with me. How fortunate is he
> who is going.

I have often thought that there's a crying need for an Arabian Chaucer to collect the Mecca Tales!

For several weeks before the pilgrims set out on their journey, there are joyful scenes up and down the country, with friends and relations gathering to wish them "God speed." In town and village there are processions of various mystical sects, with banners waving and bands playing. In some villages the entire community turns out, dressed in its best and noisy with sounds of joy. They have come to speed the departing pilgrim on his way to *Mecca el Mokarrama,* or "Mecca the Blessed." Old and young, mothers, wives, husbands and sons gather in their hundreds at country railway stations, beating drums and blowing flutes, laughing and weeping as their loved ones board the train in the first stage of their journey.

All the pilgrims arrive wearing a special dress consisting of two pieces of white material, without seam or ornament, and they continue to wear this until the celebration of the feast. In Mecca, the pilgrims perform certain traditional rites associated with Islam, and all the while this atmosphere of equality is maintained. Rich and poor, prince and peasant, assemble as equals, with no distinction of wealth or position. Many of the rites of the Pilgrimage refer back to the time of Abraham, who built the *Ka'ba* and proclaimed the Pilgrimage. It is the *Ka'ba* towards which all Moslems face while making their devotions. Among the rituals which are performed at this time is the ascent of Mount 'Arafat. It is said that, when the Angel Gabriel was showing Abraham the Pilgrim's Path and the rites of Pilgrimage, he turned to him when they reached the summit of Mount 'Arafat and said: "And now, the Pilgrims' Path is known to you," whence it derived its name. The climax of the Pilgrimage is this ascent of Mount 'Arafat on the day of the *Waqfa* or "The Standing." The "Standing" on Mount 'Arafat and the communal prayers there mark the end of the Pilgrimage, and on the following day begins the celebration of the Big Feast. Shortly after dawn on the first day of the feast, it is the custom to slaughter a sheep and to distribute the flesh among the poor and needy. This custom relates back to the time when Abraham, on God's revelation to him, offered up in sacrifice a sheep in place of his son. Many Moslem households keep the tradition, and it is quite a common sight a few days before the feast to see a sheep tethered at the entrance to houses.

And when the Pilgrimage and Feast are over, the pilgrims start on their homeward journey. By land, by sea, by air, on camel and on foot, they wend their way home. When he returns, the *Haj,* or "Pilgrim," as he will henceforth be known, is greeted with even greater rejoicing than when he left. All over the country there are homes brilliantly lit and gay with flags, with Qor'an chanting floating out on the night air. Maybe our reception of Uncle 'Ali was more subdued than this, but I think it was every bit as sincere.

In the old days, the returning pilgrim was surely full of stories about his journey, with its excitements and hazards. Nowadays, snapshots can sometimes tell the tale more eloquently, and at Uncle 'Ali's Pilgrimage Party we were soon exclaiming over scenes showing the pilgrims in their ritual dress visiting the various holy places. From some of the guests who hadn't yet made the Pilgrimage, one could detect a note of envy; from those who had there was the same look of contentment that shone from Uncle 'Ali's face. Perhaps they might even have wished to associate themselves with the thought expressed in a returning Pilgrim's song: "When shall we return to thee?"

B.B.C. "Home This Afternoon", 1968

***

If your door is low, you must bend down.

***

Moolid-el-Nabi, Birthday of the Prophet Mohammed

For the past week or two, preparations have been going on for the celebration of the Birthday of the Prophet Mohammed—the festival of *Moolid el-Nabi*. Throughout the country, bright little stalls have been springing up in the market places, attracting the children with their rows of gaily-dressed sugar dolls, horses and camels, and sweetmeats made of sesame seeds, coconut, dried split-peas, walnuts and dried fruits.

The celebration of the Prophet's Birthday takes place on the 12th day of Rabee'-el-Awwal—the third month of the Moslem calendar—and marks the anniversary of the birth of Mohammed of the Quraysh tribe in Mecca in the year 570 A.D. Since that time, the festival has been observed for very many centuries in the Moslem world, being marked by joyful celebrations in Egypt in different periods of her history. During the time of the Fatimid Dynasty, which ruled in Egypt a thousand years ago, the celebration of feasts was marked by lavish display: they loved pomp and ceremony, and it is thought most probable that it was they who introduced the colourful sugar doll, which has now become symbolic of the celebrations in Egypt.

Another addition to the observance of the festival was made five centuries ago during the reign of the Mameluke Sultan Qait Bey. (His fortress at Alexandria now houses the Maritime Museum.) On the eve of the feast, a big marquee was erected near the Citadel, in which the Sultan sat, listening to Qor'an chanters and the recital of religious songs. Largesse would then be distributed, and the following morning the Sultan distributed wheat to Soofi groups and dervishes. The Soofis are mystics and, it is said, derive their name from *soof,* the Arabic word for wool, with which the early Soofis used to clothe themselves. The Soofi tries to conduct his life according to strict Moslem principles. On this occasion, the groups meet at a central point to perform the *Zikr.* The rhythmic beating of drums gathers the members of the Soofi Order together and, when they are assembled, they walk in procession with triangular banners held aloft. On the banners are inscribed the words of the profession of faith: "There is no deity but God and Mohammed is His Messenger." In the late hours of the evening, the mystical rite of the *Zikr* begins, when the name of God is repeated rhythmically, and continues often until the early hours of the morning.

The recital of mystical poems about the Prophet Mohammed is another feature of the celebration of *Moolid-el-Nabi,* and readings are given in mosques and marqees of the Prophet's Life Story— *El Seera el Nabaweyya.* Some of these are given by *munshids* or reciters, accompanied sometimes by a flute player.

Over the centuries, many embellishments have been made to the observance of *Moolid el-Nabi,* taken from the various dynasties that have ruled in Egypt. However, like Christmas, the festival remains first and foremost a significant landmark in the religious life of the country.

The Egyptian Gazette, November, 1953

***

One hand can't clap.

Two New Year's Days in Egypt: Moslem, and Coptic

Today is Moslem New Year's Day, of the year 1372 of the *Hejra,* and tomorrow is Coptic New Year's Day of the year 1670 according to the Coptic Calendar. As the Moslem Calendar is a lunar one, and that of the Copts is solar, the difference between the two is a matter of eleven days, and it takes about thirty-three years for the Moslem Calendar to complete the cycle. The two days may not, however, be as close together as they are this year, so this occasion must be regarded as something of a rarity, and a time for rejoicing for the Moslems and Copts of Egypt.

The Moslem calendar is dated from the *Hejra,* or the migration of the Prophet Mohammed and his followers from Mecca to Medina. From earliest days these first Moslems had suffered hardship and persecution in their native city and, indeed, prior to the Hejra, some had fled for sanctuary to Abyssinia—a Christian state. Finally, their position in Mecca became untenable, and Mohammed was forced to flee, together with his loyal companion Abu Bakr, who afterwards became the first caliph in the new Islamic Commonwealth. Of this flight, many stories are told: how Mohammed and his companion were pursued by the Qoraysh tribe, to which Mohammed belonged, and how they managed eventually to elude them and continue in safety to Medina. It is said that the fugitives took refuge in a cave, and a spider spun its web across the mouth of the cave, while a dove nested at its entrance, so that the pursuers passed by, thinking the cave to be deserted. To this day, Moslems consider ungrateful any person who kills the *yemama*—that species of dove which assisted their prophet in his hour of need. It is said, too, that when Mohammed was making his way to Medina, many tribesmen came to meet him, bidding him rest and take up his abode with them. Mohammed did not stop, however, but in order not to show that he preferred any one tribe to another, he decided to choose as his home the place where his camel eventually led him.

The Moslem Calendar, dating from this migration, was not inaugurated by Mohammed himself, but during the time of the second caliph, 'Omar. Prior to this, there was no definite calendar in existence in Arabia, but dates were related to the occurrence of certain important events. For example, Mohammed was born in the "Year of the Elephant," in which an Abyssinian emperor, his army preceded by an elephant, had been defeated at Mecca, and which was therefore regarded as an important milestone in the history of the Arabs. The Moslem calendar is a lunar one, with each month containing twenty-nine or thirty days. The month which has just passed was *Zo-l-Hejja,* or the month of the Pilgrimage, and the first month of the year is *Muharram.*

The Coptic year, which begins tomorrow on the 11th of September, is a solar one, and is dated from the massacre of some Christian martyrs by the Roman Emperor Diocletian. The first month of the year is *Toot,* and the year contains twelve months of thirty days each. Five days are added at the end of the year to make up the 365 days, with of course six in a Leap Year. This follows closely the pattern of the Ancient Egyptian calendar, in which the five additional days at the end of the year represented those on which the gods Osiris, Horus, Set, Isis and Nepthys were believed to have been born. Like its forerunner of ancient times, the Coptic year is divided up for agricultural purposes into three seasons of four months each. Nowadays these are called *Shetwi*—winter, *Saifi*—summer, and *Nili*—the period of inundation, and the farmers of Egypt speak in terms of these seasons. The Ancient Egyptians called them *Shat,* or the period of sowing, *Peret,* the period of growing, and *Shomu,* the period of inundation.

At this time, when the two new years are being celebrated together in Egypt, it is interesting to see how both calendars have their specific uses and fit into the life of Egypt. The Moslem calendar is employed for religious purposes, and is based on the phases of the moon, while the Coptic calendar is used for agriculture and follows the solar cycle. Here, we can see two distinct cultures running side by side and complementing one another for, whereas the Egyptian's way of life and the agricultural round are closely linked with the solar seasons, it is the moon which has greater significance for the Arab, living his lonely desert life. The changing phases of the sun and the seasons mean little to him, for few crops grow in the sandy wastes in which he makes his home. But by night, in the clear sky over the desert, he can count the passing days and months by the waxing and waning of the moon.

And when the moon is down, he is guided on his way by the thousand eyes of night.

When Egypt adopted Islam as her religion, she took the Arabic calendar for religious purposes, but for agriculture she retained the one used, in effect, since ancient times. And so the Arab and the Egyptian ways of life fused together, the one having its roots in the barren desert and the other in the fertile plains. These two entirely different cultures and philosophies have flowed together to produce this modern land of Egypt.

The Egyptian Gazette, September, 1953

* * *

*Find out about your neighbour
before you buy a house.*

* * *

Christmas in Egypt

Christmas in Egypt makes the best of many worlds as there are several Christian communities in Egypt, and each celebrates the feast in its own special way and on different days. The Egyptian Christians, or Copts as they are generally known, observe Christmas on the 7th of January. It is almost exclusively a religious feast for the Copts—preceded by a month of fasting—although many have adopted the custom of giving presents. Other Orthodox Christians also observe Christmas on the 7th of January, or on the 6th as the Armenian Church does. Catholics and Protestants, of course, observe December 25th as Christmas Day. And so for two whole weeks it is Christmas in Egypt, and one gets used to people wishing one a happy Christmas—*Kol sana w'entom tayyebeen,* "May you be well and happy every year"—on any day until the 7th of January.

Christmas is a very popular festival in Egypt, and not only with Christians. The shops are gaily decorated: there are all kinds of Christmas cards on sale—with a pyramids motif rather than a snow scene, or perhaps a pharaoh receiving offerings; Christmas trees grown in desert-reclaimed land line some of the fashionable streets, and Egyptians enjoy decorating them as much as anybody else. Many children of Moslem families who go to foreign-language schools have introduced Western Christmas ideas, and it is not at all unusual to see a Christmas tree in a Moslem household: and of course the children encourage the idea of present-giving! They join in with carols too, and there are special shows for the season—if not an actual pantomime. Some years ago Benjamin Britten's "Let's make an Opera" was performed in Arabic at Cairo Opera House, and was greatly enjoyed by both the Arabic-speaking and non-Arabic-speaking audience. Again, recently, a dazzling pantomime-style show based on a famous classical Arabic work was performed by the Egyptian Organization of Theatre and Music at the Nile-side Balloon Theatre; anybody looking for a lavish show, with excellent staging and decor, glamorous costumes and a colourful Egyptian atmosphere of good humour would surely have enjoyed this performance at festival time. The visitor may also have the opportunity of seeing shows by folklore dancers at the Balloon Theatre and probably a puppet show at the Cairo Puppet Theatre.

For decorating the house at Christmas time, there is the beautiful red poinsettia plant, which grows in profusion in Egypt. It is known here as "daughter of the consul," as it is often grown in embassy and consulate gardens. There are masses of roses, too, for roses are at their best at this time of the year, while splendid white chrysanthemums are used to fine effect to give the traditional Christmas contrast of red and white.

The Christmas story is at one's very doorstep in Egypt. At Heliopolis, or "City of the Sun," or "New Cairo," as it is variously known, there is an ancient sycamore tree where the Holy Family are believed to have rested on their flight into Egypt. Standing to the northeast of Cairo, Heliopolis was once a centre for sun worship in Egypt, and it is said that when the infant Jesus was brought into the Temple of the Sun, the idols fell.

The Holy Family probably came into Egypt by the old caravan route across the desert, and on their way southwards, they stopped at the place now known as Old Cairo, very near the Nile. There, the visitor will find the Church of Saint Sergius, and will be shown the crypt, about thirty feet below street level which, according to tradition, was built on the site of the place where the Holy Family sheltered. At the Coptic Museum close by, there is a famous icon known as "The Flight into Egypt," showing the infant Jesus on the shoulder of Joseph and beside him a donkey bearing the Virgin

Mary. An so, with its close link with the first Christmas, Egypt welcomes the visitor celebrating the festival in this ancient land.

The Egyptian Gazette, December, 1953
B.B.C. "Home This Afternoon," December, 1969

***
The one who comes late has his excuse with him.

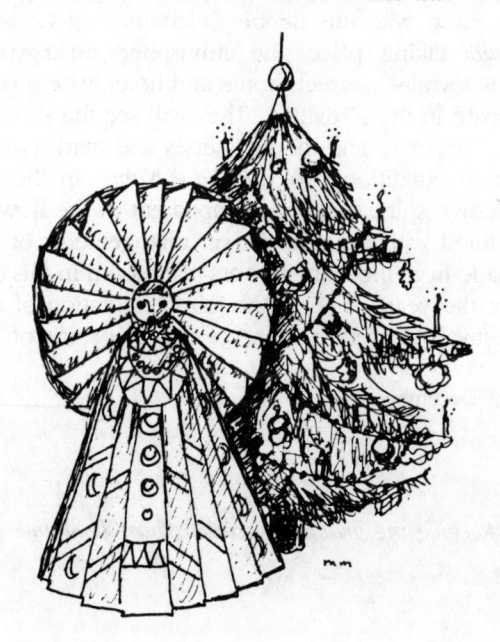

Christmas and Moolid-el-Nabi together

The scene in Egypt this December is bound to be particularly bright and cheerful, because two of the most important festivals of the country are being celebrated, and within two days of each other! Western Christmas of Catholics and Protestants is, of course, a fixed date, observed on the 25th of December, but the other festival, *Moolid-el-Nabi*—Birthday of the Prophet Mohammed—follows the Islamic lunar calendar and comes this year two days after Western Christmas.

Moolid-el-Nabi has been especially remarkable this year as, because of varying eleven days each year, it has been observed twice during 1982. The previous time, on January 7th, created a most amazing coincidence, coming on the same day as Christmas of the Copts. When this happened last January, it gave rise to many commentaries in the Egyptian press on its symbolic nature, drawing attention to the unity of Egypt's two main religious groups.

And so now, with this double celebration of Christmas and *Moolid-el-Nabi* taking place, the atmosphere in Egypt in late December is joyful—in street, home and hotel, where visitors too may participate in the festivities. They will see the shops brightly dressed for Christmas, and the patisseries and markets filled with the sweetmeats traditional for *Moolid-el-Nabi*. In the shopping areas, the festive spirit is especially apparent in the flower shops, which are filled with beautiful flower arrangements of all kinds, skillfully made from the many flowers that bloom in this country at this time of the year. Indeed, the joint celebration of these two religious festivals conveys a sense of the true spirit of Egypt.

Cairo Today, December, 1982

***

Receive me graciously rather than feed me.

THE ANTIQUITIES

Introduction

The work of the Egyptologists continues, but the change in the scene again is that brought about by the building of both the Aswan Dam and High Dam. This has necessitated extensive work in removing and restoring monuments affected by the new level of the Nile and rising subsoil waters. Most noteworthy of these were the monuments at Abu Simbel, beyond the High Dam, which were threatened with submersion by the new height of the river, and the removal of which to a new site higher up the river bank was undertaken by international cooperation through UNESCO, in view of the priceless nature of this cultural heritage. Another big project necessitated by the building of the High Dam was that undertaken on the Temple of Isis at Philae, referred to in the articles on Luxor and Aswan and that on Egyptology. These are but two examples of the work being done to preserve the Egyptian antiquities for posterity—a task which continues unceasingly throughout the year.

***

Luxor and Aswan

"Luxor and Aswan." There is a strange fascination in the names themselves, and the visions they conjure up in the imagination. Before I visited Upper Egypt I had often studied the posters of the Egyptian Tourism Department, with their inviting views of the Karnak temples, the Colossi of Memnon, the tombs and temples of Thebes, the Nile at Aswan. Often, too, on railway journeys, I had stared idly at the advertisement on the sides of the compartment: "HAVE YOU VISITED THE MARVELLOUS REMAINS OF EGYPT'S ANCIENT CIVILISATION?", and my imagination had woven pictures of the wonders I might discover when I journeyed southwards. When, eventually, the opportunity came for me to visit these legendary places, I was to find that the reality was infinitely more marvellous than the dream. I was also to realize that I had not known this land of the Nile, nor understood its true nature, until I visited Luxor and Aswan.

Everywhere in Egypt the Nile is beautiful, but probably nowhere so beautiful as at Aswan, where it passes majestically over the Cataracts and the many small islands dotted in its path. And probably nowhere in Egypt is one made so aware of the importance of the river to the life of the country and the utter dependence of the Egyptians throughout history on its rising and falling. In ancient times, it was believed that, from the rocks of the first cataract, the water flowed northwards and southwards—that there was the source of the Nile.

It was also believed that the risings of the river were controlled by the god Khnum, who was the local deity of Aswan in ancient times. He was the ram-headed god, the moulder of mankind, who is often depicted on tomb and temple walls moulding kings and commoners on his potter's wheel. He is to be seen in the reliefs at

Luxor Temple and Deir el Bahari, showing the divine births of Queen Hatshepsut and Amenhotep III.

When I visited Elephantine Island, which lies in the centre of the river opposite Aswan, and which was the home of Khnum, I was to understand yet another of the beliefs of the Ancient Egyptians. It was nightfall when I visited the Island of Khnum. The moon had not yet risen, and the frogs chanted a contented chorus from among the many small rocks that dotted the river. The Nubian sailor pulled skilfully on his oars, with a sure knowledge of the shallows and channels through which we made our way. As we jumped ashore, we were conscious of our feet sinking slightly in the earth, and suddenly I remembered that this was the "clay Aswanli" which Egyptian sculptors use for modelling. I remembered too, that this was the home of Khnum, the moulder of mankind and, in remembering, yet one more belief of the Ancient Egyptians became linked with the present and understood.

Aswan can tell us much about the story of Egypt, for it has been an important centre throughout all periods of her history. For thousands of years it has been the connection between the northern and southern parts of the Valley, and in the colourful market can be found the produce of Egypt, Nubia and the Sudan. In early times, Aswan was the starting point for expeditions southwards, into Central Africa, and high up on the hills dominating the town are the tombs of the adventurous explorers and caravan-leaders of long ago. These tombs have not the splendour and beauty of those of the kings and queens and nobles at Thebes, but they tell a tale of the courage and spirit of adventure of the men who ventured on hazardous expeditions for the glory of their country.

But though Aswan has a long and fascinating history, extending back through the Islamic civilisation, the Coptic and Greco-Roman periods, back into early Pharaonic times, yet the name Aswan has a modern ring to it, and indeed it is impossible now to speak of Aswan without calling to mind the great dam which spans the river just above the Cataracts. This huge dam of pink granite has completely changed the life of Egypt, providing countless new areas for cultivation, and enabling the ground to be planted with three different crops each year instead of only one, as in the past. The great dam, with the water pouring from the sluice-gates, sparkling in the brilliant sunshine and catching the light to form an ever-present rainbow, is a magnificent and awe-inspiring sight, not soon to be forgotten.

For the Ancient Egyptians, as with their descendants of modern times, one of the main attractions of Aswan was the superb pink granite which is quarried not far from the town. This granite, of which the dam is built, has been used by Egyptians throughout the centuries for their statues, their temples and their monuments. These quarries provided the material for the statues of Ramses II in ancient times, and for Moukhtar's present-day statue of "The Awakening of Egypt," which stands at the approach to Cairo University. In ancient times, the great blocks of granite were ferried downstream to the capital of the empire at Thebes, and for those of us who have watched the graceful felukas making their way northwards, with their cargoes of stone building material, clay drinking vessels, cotton and wheat, it is not difficult to imagine the river craft of ancient times carrying the precious granite from Aswan to Thebes—now more generally known as Luxor.

Nor is it difficult to visualize the great imperial capital of Thebes in ancient times, and today, some three thousand five hundred years later, it still retains the atmosphere of its past splendour. Much of the great temples of Karnak and Luxor still remains, their statues and paintings calling up visions of the scenes of rejoicing, prayer and thanksgiving which were enacted within the sacred walls. Recent excavations have brought to light the Avenue of Sphinxes, starting from the Festival Temple of Amon-Ra, from the earth and buildings under which it has lain for centuries. Now we can see before us in its ancient glory the avenue down which the priests carried the sacred boat of Amon-Ra after the festival celebrations at the Temple of Luxor, and we can re-create in imagination the feasts of the inundation, of spring and harvest-time which marked the Ancient Egyptian year.

Across the river lies the City of the Dead, where are buried the pharaohs, their queens and the noblemen of their courts. At Luxor, we can easily understand that it was natural that the Ancient Egyptians should worship the sun, just as it was natural that they should choose as their last resting-place the rugged hills behind which their sun-god disappeared each evening. And when we cross the river to the Valley of the Kings and Queens, we can feel in the tombs a marvellous atmosphere of peace and serenity. Here, in mbs, in glorious colours, are depicted scenes from the lives of the ancient Egyptians, which tell us that these people did not fear death, but rather looked upon it as a continuation of an earthly existence which they had found utterly delightful.

It was, indeed, at Thebes that I came to realize the full beauty and splendour of Egypt. The rising sun is reflected on the western hills in the "City of the Dead," and they become suffused with a pink glory that is caught and held by the unruffled surface of the river. At sunset, the hills are etched against an orange backcloth as the great Ra, sun-god of the Ancient Egyptians, disappears over the western horizon. And as I stood beside the temple of Amon-Ra, there rose before my eyes a vision of the past, when the temple grounds were gay with flower-gardens, when the pharaoh and his priests marched in solemn procession down the great Avenue of Sphinxes, and when the hymns of praise of the assembled throng drifted out from the temple precincts across the waters of the life-giving river. As I stood there, rapt in thought, the voice of the mu'azzin floated out from the near-by mosque—out over the temple courts, over the stately columns and statues of a by-gone age. Another day was over; once more the sun had passed into other regions and it was night; once more the people were called to prayer, to ask God for His mercy and protection, and to thank Him for His many blessings.

Egyptian Radio, 1952

***

What brings you to God is allowed.

Why not be an Egyptologist?

When the young Egyptian student of history looks around him and wonders what career to choose, there lies before him, at his very door-step, one of the most fascinating professions of modern times—the study of the past of this ancient land, the science of Egyptology.

There are, no doubt, many people who fail to see any value in digging up the past. Such people might agree that existing monuments are interesting for the tourist, but would argue that any further excavations are out of place in an age which is so engrossed with its own struggle for survival. There may be some truth in such beliefs, for we live in troubled times and it may seem as mere escapism to bury oneself in the past as do the Egyptologists. But, in fact, their science is not a dead one, for their researches are helping to tell the story of Egypt and its ancient civilisation. And if we care to study the beliefs and way of life of these people from their earliest recorded history, we can learn much that will help us to solve our problems of today. To the Egyptologist, in fact, his subject is a very living one, and I have always found these scientists to speak with the greatest fervour about their work.

The antiquities are one of Egypt's leading attractions, and have been so since the time when the Napoleonic Expedition first interested Europe in this part of the world. Since those early days, the science of Egyptology has branched off from archaeology, and the subject has attracted scholars from many different countries, as well as providing a study for Egyptian scholars themselves. The Antiquities Department of the Egyptian Government covers a very wide field of study and research, as well as excavation of new sites, maintenance of existing antiquities, and restoration. It was not until I had the opportunity of visiting Upper Egypt that I came to realize the immense scope of the work of the Antiquities Department, and how much care is taken to preserve for future generations the wonderful records of Egypt's past civilizations which the sands and the sunshine have preserved for us.

Many people imagine that the Antiquities Department is only concerned with excavating new sites—always hoping, of course, for some world-shaking discovery—and then transporting the finds to the museum. It may be realized that there is a certain amount of maintenance work to be done, and seeing to it that the ever-encroaching desert sands do not claim again the treasures that have been wrested from them. These may have been the limits of the work of the Egyptologist in the early days, but since that time—in the very early days of this century—a new element has appeared which has changed the whole scene. This new factor is the Aswan Dam, completed in 1902, which spans the river just above the Cataracts, and which has had such a great influence on the lives of the people of the Nile Valley. The dam, mighty both in its conception and its effect, together with the many other irrigation schemes, has brought new life to the land but is playing a big part in destroying the antiquities. The Antiquities Department, therefore, is waging an unending struggle against the rising sub-soil waters and the dampness which the new irrigation schemes have brought in their wake. Nowadays, when we visit the different antiquities centres, we are shown not only the temples, monuments and tombs, but also the steps being taken to combat the enemy waters and their destructive effects. At Abydos, ancient centre for Osiris worship, work has been going on for several years to strengthen the walls of the beautiful temple of Pharaoh Seti I, which the sub-soil waters have been eating away. In the City of the Dead in the western hills at Luxor, there is restoration work in progress in some of the tombs, where the dampness has affected the rich colourings of these royal burial places. Most people will have heard of the legend that a curse was laid upon anyone who forced his way into these sacred precincts, but whether such a curse was ever called down or whether anybody suffered harm as a result of this curse is hypothetical. It is certain, however, that the pharaohs, their architects and artists, feared the breaking open of these sealed and silent chambers, and the despoilation that would follow; it is less likely that they realized the destruction that the air would cause once the seals were broken.

Though not many people have been aware of the insidious effects of the dampness caused by the many irrigation schemes, and of the struggle of the Antiquities Department to preserve its treasures, they may have heard of the submerged island of Philae, just beyond the Aswan Dam, and may have paused for a moment's sad reflection that the noble temple of Isis lies beneath the Nile waters for most of the year. It is only between July and October, when the dam opens its vents and the flood waters pour down over the valley, that we can see again the beautiful temple of Isis and monuments relating to the Pharaonic, Ptolemaic and Roman periods. Each year, when the waters recede, the Antiquities Department sends its inspectors and architects to examine the sites and perform the necessary strengthening and repairs. But each year, more of the ancient glory is gone, the former beauty only a memory, and apart from its academic interest, Philae is lost.

There is no doubt that Egyptology is a fascinating and absorbing science, but sometimes one is curious to know how different people first became attracted to this subject, and how their interest was first aroused. Each member of the Antiquities Department has his own special reason for taking up the profession: one perhaps because he had always been drawn to the subject since his first visit to the Egyptian Museum in the time of his boyhood; another because of the sort of life that Egyptology offered him—travelling about all over the country, studying the different areas and spending a great deal of time in the open air on excavation work; yet another, who is both an artist and an architect, has found that the profession offers him satisfying scope for both these interests. I remember in Luxor discovering yet another reason why Egyptology exercises such a strong attraction: it is the knowledge that it brings that the past and the present are one—that they are bound together by habits and customs which may modify with the times, but which do not change fundamentally. In Luxor, the charming house of the Antiquities Inspectorate faces the river on one side, and on another the general hospital. One morning, as I neared the Inspectorate, the eerie wailing of lamentation was heard, and outside the hospital gates a small group of peasants had gathered, mourning in their own characteristic way the passing of one of their folk. Their cries were harsh and un-nerving, and under the shade of a near-by tree, the bereaved son was rocking himself backwards and forwards in an agony of sorrow. "*Ya abuya, ya abuya,*"—"My father, my father," he moaned. Inside the Inspectorate, the Chief Inspector of Antiquities in the area, Dr. Labib Habashy, was eyeing the scene from his window. There was a strange expression on his face, and his eyes were bright. "It's all the same, just the same," he said. "Nothing has changed in all these thousands of years. That mourner under the tree, rocking himself backwards and forwards—the movement, the pose: everything was the same in the days of the pharaohs. Surely there is nothing new under the sun."

The Egyptian Gazette, October, 1953

***

The worst ordeal is that which makes you laugh.

***

A Day at the Excavations

During my many years of living in Egypt I have been fortunate enough to go on excavation trips with Egyptologists, and have found the experience to be an altogether delightful one. First of all, there is the excitement—the hope that this time there is going to be some important discovery made, or some precious treasures found; then there is the enjoyment itself of driving through the fertile countryside to where the desert meets the sown, and climbing up onto the desert plateau through the rocks and sand dunes to the excavation site. And of course there is the interest of the way the excavations are carried out, and how the Egyptologist and his team of assistants and workers proceed.

One of the expeditions I took part in was to the valley temple of the Pharaoh Senefru, father of the builder of the Great Pyramid at Giza. This whole pyramid complex is at Dahshur, on the desert plateau between Saqqara and Giza. Senefru's pyramid, dating back to about 2,800 B.C., has a strange bent shape, and stands out as a clear landmark, like the Step Pyramid of Zoser and the three Great Pyramids themselves. Excavations had been going on for several seasons, I was told, because there had been some doubt as to whose pyramid complex this was. But apparently the problem had been solved through examination of carvings on the temple, and the frequent appearance of the pharaoh's name in the royal cartouche. This having been established, the next step was to excavate the site, to find records of the life of the pharaoh and his contemporaries and perhaps, with luck, some treasures which had escaped the ubiquitous tomb-robber!

It was a golden winter day when we set out through the countryside, the waters of the irrigation canals sparkling in the sunshine. On the fringes separating the cultivated land from the desert, the peasants were stacking the dried stalks of the cotton crop for firewood. As we drove up to the site of the excavations, we found the workmen busily removing the drift sand from the recently-discovered valley temple. While they did so they sang. That is the custom with workmen in Egypt. This singing in chorus lightens the monotony of the work and also gives the desired rhythm. The foreman signals to the chorus leader, who puts down his spade, goes to a position dominating the scene, and begins to sing. The first song welcomes the beginning of the day's work.

> O Almighty God,
> Thou, who art the beginning of all things,
> And who giveth the people abundance,
> And upon whom we depend for our daily bread,
> We begin our day asking for Thy help.

When we came nearer, we were soon able to pick out the chorus leaders. There were two: one was a Bedouin who apparently had a great reputation in the western desert both for his poems and musical compositions—a true descendant of desert poets like 'Antara and Qais, who have found poetry their best means of expression. This Bedouin chorus-leader was dressed in a flowing robe, with a silk patterned scarf wound round his shoulders. His technique was to sit quietly on a jutting piece of rock while the workmen chanted their familiar choruses; then he would suddenly rise to his feet and sing a few lines that he had just composed and the workers would quickly pick up the new melody and chant the chorus. At times, the Bedouin poet would take out his flute and accompany the singers.

If this first chorus leader at the excavations at Dahshur called to mind the Arab strain in Egyptian culture, the other was more reminiscent of his Pharaonic ancestors. Indeed, he might have stepped right out of one of the bas-reliefs on the monuments he was helping to uncover. He wore a short tunic, and round his waist was a light brown girdle, looped and falling to the lower edge of the tunic. He sang with spirit in his warm, pleasant voice, and his comrades joined in the choruses. Most of the workers' songs were bright and cheerful, and some spoke of love. One of them addressed the beloved, harvesting wheat in the fields in the valley:

> O beautiful one,
> Embrace in your arms
> The sheaves of wheat.

As the workers bore their baskets of drift-sand on their shoulders to the waiting truck, the scene they created was remarkably like some of those on the walls of Senefru's temple which they had been unearthing.

While the excavations continued and the workers sang, we were entertained in traditional Bedouin manner. One of the permanent watchmen came from a nearby tent, bearing a tray with minute glasses, containing the very sweet brewed tea drunk by the Bedouin—and, indeed, by most Egyptians. As we stood sipping our tea, gazing at the vast panorama of desert and rolling dunes, we were suddenly startled by a gun report close at hand. Apparently the workers had been singing the praises of the Pharaoh Senefru. At the mention of his name, the watchman had fired a shot in salute, and a few seconds later the mention of our famous Egyptologist friend, Dr. Ahmed Fakhry, formerly professor at Cairo University, whose work had helped to reveal so much about this pharaoh of the Pyramid Age, called forth another salute.

Everybody taking part in the dig seemed to enjoy himself thoroughly. Apart from their gay singing, the workers were as excited as anybody when their spades turned over some object of interest. That day, some small pottery bowls and vases had been found, and a *Ushepti* figurine—one of those buried with the deceased and intended to do his work for him in the next world! Certainly nobody was more thrilled than the Egyptologist himself. Speaking to us about his work, he exclaimed enthusiastically: "You know, these people whose temples I'm working on aren't dead to me; they're with me always. I feel these pharaohs and their subjects, the priests and vizirs, are alive and part of myself. I'm never lonely when I have such wonderful companions."

Soon, the winter sun was getting low in the sky, and the workers knew it was nearly time to down tools for the day. Many of them had some distance to walk home and were anxious to be on their way before dusk. At four o'clock a gong sounded, and the workers quickly collected their belongings from beside the tent and, breaking up into little groups, strode swiftly over the sands. Some more fortunate ones trotted off on their donkeys, which had waited patiently throughout the day as their owners worked and sang. The little groups fanned out, taking their various routes through the dunes and down into the valley, some workers still humming the songs of the day's toil. A few of the men took up their posts to guard the excavations during the night. Soon all was quiet, and we prepared to make our homeward journey down from the desert plateau. By now, the sun had gone down and the desert had taken on its mysterious, purple look, and the Bent Pyramid of Senefru was silhouetted against the sky, keeping its lonely vigil as it has done for the past five thousand years.

B.B.C. "Woman's Hour," June, 1972

ASPECTS OF EGYPT

Introduction

In this section, it is important for the reader to notice the date of the particular item, in order to appreciate that certain changes may have taken place since it was written. For example, "The Changing Status of Women" was broadcast in 1968, and the situation has obviously changed since then. The extract on "Women Pioneers," however, develops the story, bringing it further up to date. Of the other subjects included in this section, perhaps the only one that shows change of any importance is that concerning "The Street Vendors of Cairo". This broadcast was given in 1948, and since then life in Egypt has changed considerably, and many of these picturesque figures have disappeared from the scene, appearing nowadays in folklore shows and television, though some of their songs are, unfortunately, lost for ever. Here again, the broadcast comparing buskers and street vendors of London and Cairo gives a more up-to-date picture.

***

The Changing Status of Women

When I first went to Egypt over twenty years ago as the bride of an Egyptian, I surprised my very conservative in-laws by deciding to take a job. My father-in-law, who was a retired Judge of Appeal, was quite sure I was doing this merely to pass the time: his own two daughters had stayed at home after taking their school-leaving certificate and spent their time paying social calls, making their own clothes, doing embroidery, and generally helping their mother in the house—although there were servants to do most of the work. Their case was typical: very few Egyptian girls continued their education beyond school-leaving; most clerical office jobs were done by foreigners who knew French and English well, and the universities and colleges of further education had only a sprinkling of women at that time—and they were regarded as rather a curiosity!

How different is the picture today—twenty years later! At the American University where I teach English as a foreign language, girl students equal the men, and in some courses, such as English literature, far out-number them. There is a large proportion of married women students who have come back to study, like their peers in England, once their children have passed their dependent stage. These so-called "mature students" are, in fact, mostly still very young, for they married in their late teens, as was the custom, had their children, and then were only too anxious to take up their studies where they had left off, both for economic reasons and also to fulfil their intellectual needs—neglected for so long in past generations. The women students have distinguished themselves, too: on the platform at the Honours Assembly last semester there was a predominance of women students—a remarkable, but increasingly typical situation in a country where for so many centuries men have dominated the scene. It is the same in the other universities and colleges and in the business world too, where educated Egyptian women, with their knowledge of classical Arabic, have taken over the jobs from foreigners, for Arabic is now used in business concerns as well as government offices, and it is no longer sufficient to know only English and French.

A few years before the Egyptian Revolution in 1952, I was very struck by the fact that women radio announcers were reading out the election results, although they themselves had not the right to vote! It was women like these who were among the pioneers of women's rights in Egypt. The first of these pioneers was a lady of aristocratic family, Hoda Sha'rawy, who some forty years ago arrived back from a European holiday, and instead of putting on her *yashmak* on landing in Egypt—as had been the custom—drove to her home with unveiled face. Since that time, the women of Egypt have fought and won the battle for their emancipation and have invaded every profession. A few years ago a woman held the office of Minister of Social Affairs and at a conference on Women and Careers she said that "beauty alone can no longer open doors; work is an inevitable necessity for women in present-day society." (This post has continued to be held by a woman.) Here, of course, one must remember that the vast majority of the women of Egypt *have* always worked: the peasant women have always worked side by side with their menfolk in the fields, quite apart from looking after the house, baking the bread and caring for their numerous children. Even here, though, change is apparent: the village people are now well aware of the value of educating their children and the dearest wish of a peasant woman for her daughter would doubtless be that she should have the education that she herself had missed.

The woman in the small provincial towns in Egypt has been very much governed by conservative oriental traditions, and for generations has been entirely secluded from social life, living only for her home and children and cut off from any social activity. Here, too, there have been rapid changes in recent years, with women members of parliament coming from this stronghold of conservatism. In televised scenes of local elections, it has been really fascinating to see Egyptian women of every walk of life coming to the polls: a shrivelled old crone from the village, the President's wife with her sweet, unaffected smile, groups of pretty young students, a working-class wife wearing her traditional black sheet-like garment wound concealingly around her body: it is called *melayya-leff,* "sheet wrapping," and the wearing of it seems to be one of the most rigidly clung-to conventions of this class of society.

My maid—a twice-married woman with six children—will on no account be persuaded to give up her *melayya-leff* in spite of the pleas of her children and myself, and the fact that it has nearly tripped her under the wheels of the over-crowded bus on several occasions when she has been hurrying to work. She finds several arguments in its favour which prevent her giving it up: in the first place, it acts as an overcoat, protecting its wearer and any baby that a woman of this class is so often carrying; in the second place, anything can be worn underneath it, summer or winter, and kept clean from the dusty or muddy streets. But most important of all, it would shame her in the eyes of all her neighbourhood if she were to discard it, for the garment is surely the last vestige of the all-concealing shroud with which oriental women used to conceal themselves from the eyes of curious menfolk, (and still do in some places) and therefore constitutes a symbol of respectability in this age of fast-disappearing conventions. Indeed, what *would* the neighbours say if she left off her *melayya-leff?* My maid took only her primary school certificate, leaving school at twelve and marrying at fourteen. Her sisters were more fortunate and have continued their education to technical college and university; her children, too, have similar futures planned for them.

Women in Egypt have certainly come a long way since they emerged from the hareem and the veil, but they do still lead a very sheltered existence compared with their western sisters. Of course, it is not nearly so strict as in the past, when all marriages were arranged and it was quite often the case for a bride to see her husband for the first time on their wedding day. Nowadays, although there is undoubtedly a great amount of marriage-arranging, I think it fair to say that the majority of educated girls do choose their own husbands. But even so, there is little or no "dating" of the sort known in the West; the only meetings between un-engaged couples take place at college or office or club, and it is only when they are engaged that they are allowed to be seen out together in public. Convention dies very hard indeed in this respect, and in the more remote regions in Upper Egypt and the oases, observation of tradition is still very strict indeed.

The relationship between the sexes at university and business appears to be a wholesome one, governed as it is by the traditions of the society. Some people feel that the influence of western films is dangerous, with their emphasis on sex, crime and violence, but apart from copying some of the fashions and following the latest "pop" hits, most Egyptian girls take a rather detached attitude towards such themes, regarding them as aspects of an alien society with completely different moral values.

Egypt has had many remarkable women in her history. Nearly everybody knows of the beautiful Nefertiti, consort of the first monotheistic king in history, Akhenaton; Cleopatra, too, is legendary for her personality and her influence on history. Hatshepsut of Ancient Egypt was another of the same calibre, ruling as a queen in her own right and wearing the beard of kingship to show her equality with men. Shagaret-el-Dorr or "Tree of Pearls" was a queen of the Mameluke era in the 13th century who greatly influenced the history of her country. With such figures as these for inspiration, it is not surprising that the modern Egyptian woman has fought for her rights and, having attained them in many respects, she is determined to make her full contribution to the life of the country.

B.B.C. "Woman's Hour", 1968.

***

If the grain were as much as the husk,
the mother-in-law would love her daughter-in-law.

Women Pioneers

Looking back over the past few months, one cannot fail to mention the ceremony held in Cairo in March marking the United Nations-sponsored International Day for Woman. The ceremony was organized by the Society of Hoda Sha'rawy, who pioneered the emancipation of women in the first decade of this century. The ceremony was held at the Meridien Hotel, and certificates were presented by the Minister of Insurance and Social Affairs, Dr. Amal 'Osman (herself a woman) to the twenty-one women pioneers who, as the magazine *Akher Sa'a* put it, "stormed" work in many fields and proved their excellence, opening the way to other women and becoming an example, followed by many after them in journalism, broadcasting, letters, social work, medicine, aviation, acting and cinema direction. The certificate, which was prepared by the Meridien Hotel, carries a message, thanking the recipient for the effort and energy she gave to Egypt in the position she occupies. It is written on papyrus, with a painting of the montheist pharaoh Akhenaton and his family for illustration.

An example showing the change in attitude since the early pioneering days is the case of Dr. 'Aisha Mourad, one of the recipients of the certificate. When she first had the opportunity to go to England in the early 1930's, her mother apparently determinedly stood in her way. With her own daughter, however, a generation later, it was quite a different story, and 'Aisha Mourad gave every encouragement to Magda to continue her career in ballet and to spend eight years in Moscow, studying with the Bolshoi Ballet Company. Magda's thesis for her Doctorate was based on the study of pharaonic dances as depicted in ancient Egyptian murals.

Other pioneers mentioned in a book by Charis Waddy on *Women in Moslem History* and honoured at the ceremony at the Meridien Hotel are Seza Nabarawy who, with Hoda Sha'rawy, led the movement for the liberation of Egyptian women, 'Aziza Hussein, a leading figure in social work in Egypt, including the Cairo Family Planning Association, of which she is chairman, Amina el-Sa'eed, a leading journalist, and Dr. Soheir el Qalamawy, the first woman to enter the field of university education and to rise to become a university professor and head of the Department of Arabic at Cairo University.

At this point, it is certainly worthwhile to note some of the positions of authority held by women in Egypt today. The heads of Television and Radio are women, as are those of the Departments of Music and Opera, the Conservatoire and Ballet. The Ambassador to West Germany is a woman, as is the Minister of Social Affairs. The head of the Department of English at Cairo University is a woman, and also of the National Theatre, while there are many prominent women doctors, lawyers, engineers and banking experts.

Cairo Today, May, 1982

***

The legs of those who are deficient in reason get tired.

***

Health and Beauty in Egypt

One of the first things to impress the visitor to Egypt must surely be the supple grace and beauty of the people, their healthy appearance, the flashing brilliance of their teeth, and the rich luxuriousness of their hair. The fact is that, apart from the natural grace of an agricultural people, the pursuance of health and beauty has been a cult in Egypt since earliest times, and this cult has continued to exist, consciously or otherwise, down to present times. It was the Egyptians who, more than fifty centuries ago, laid the foundations of medical science; it was they who first realized the healing value of herbs and passed on their knowledge and the results of their experimentation to subsequent generations, who understood the importance of cleanliness for health and built pools and baths in their homes for this purpose, who were great sportsmen and delighted in all forms of health-giving open air sport and exercise, as any study of Ancient Egyptian painting will reveal.

Nowadays, modern hygiene decrees that health and cleanliness are synonymous. Though this belief has not always prevailed in the world, yet with the Egyptians cleanliness has been highly revered throughout the ages. In ancient times down to present days, bathing, for example, has been a practice regularly indulged in and enjoyed by the Egyptians. As the famous Egyptologist E.A. Wallis

Budge records in *The Dwellers on the Nile*, "Egyptians attached the greatest importance to personal cleanliness." Thus it has continued down through the centuries and today we are still able to find evidences of the importance attached to bathing if we visit some of the charming houses of the seventeenth and eighteenth centuries in Cairo and observe the facilities provided in those days for bathing, massage and the like—considered essential for a healthy and graceful body. For those who had not the luxury of a bath in their own homes, public bathing was the thing to do and the weekly, or bi-weekly visit to the baths became an outstanding social event, about which several European visitors of that time have written. In particular, Edward William Lane devotes a chapter to "The Bath" in *The Modern Egyptians*, saying "Bathing is one of the greatest luxuries enjoyed by the people of Egypt."

Apart from the pleasure the Egyptians derive from bathing and their frequent indulgence in the habit, cleanliness in general represents one very important aspect of the Moslem religion. Ablutions are prescribed before each period of devotions—that is, five times a day—and the religion is such a living thing in the lives of people that even those who do not make a regular practice of performing their devotions are well aware of the injunction to cleanliness and fulfill this duty accordingly. Moreover, in the past and even nowadays many Egyptians rely on their hands rather than on knives and forks for eating purposes, and this practice has caused them to be scrupulously careful in washing hands and mouth before and after meals. Here again, custom is so strong that, even where knife and fork have been adopted, the washing habit continues.

A final word in this connection. The belief in the use of running water rather than standing water has always been very strong in the East. Running water carries away impurities, and anybody who has observed the employment of this principle in Egypt in the washing of eating and drinking utensils must have realized its value for health. It can be seen, for example, in the fruit-juice shops, where glasses are carefully washed in running water before re-use for sugar-cane, mango, or guava juice.

But while cleanliness in general is so necessary for the preservation of health, sickness and disease are part of the human lot, and when preventive methods fail, curative measures must be employed. Here again we go back to the Ancient Egyptians for the first medical experimentation and use of herbs for healing. In classical times the Egyptians had a great reputation for medical knowledge, and documentary evidence of their achievements is provided by the famous *Medical Papyri*, which cover many different aspects of the subject—such as medical and household recipes, surgery and gynaecology, and so on. In the first place, the practice of embalming the dead had a great influence upon the development of medicine, as Warren R. Dawson says in the chapter on medicine in *The Legacy of Egypt*, as it familiarized the Egyptians with the appearance, nature and positions of the internal organs of the body—an opportunity denied to other peoples, where religion and popular prejudice had forbidden the dissection of the human body. The second great contribution to medicine made by the Ancient Egyptians was the experimentation with and use of herbs, and these first recipes have been passed on through succeeding generations, down to the present day. Magic played a prominent part in the life of the Ancient Egyptians, and it was to the accompaniment of magical rituals and incantations that the earliest use of herbs was made, records Warren Dawson.

Nowadays, though the services of the modern equivalent of the magician—the physician—are much sought after, yet the Egyptians still retain a remarkable knowledge of herbs and their uses for everyday ailments. The chemist's preparations may have high-sounding names and be contained in elegant bottles and colourful wrappers, but this again, the Egyptian well knows, is only part of the magician's art and many of them, he is aware, are the same country herbs known and used by him and his mother and grandmother before him. For that universal malady the common cold, whose origin still baffles the scientists, the Egyptian housewife will brew for you cinnamon or linseed; for stomach disorders there is garlic, which is widely employed in cooking, caraway, korkoom—the herb which gives curry its yellow colour—or nutmeg. If you have toothache you will be given henbane or beng—which is the Egyptian word for anaesthetic, implying something which renders one unconscious to pain. And in this connection, nobody knows better than the Egyptian how to safeguard the health of his teeth. Long before the advent of that modern contrivance, the tooth-brush, he was using a similarly-shaped implement called a *miswak*, cut from a small tree-branch, the juices of which are very beneficial to the teeth. Nor is chewing-gum a novelty to the Egyptian, and probably for many centuries before this habit was popularized in the New World he was chewing *liban*, which is a tree-resin serving not only to strengthen the teeth and refresh the mouth, but also to aid digestion. After meals he cleans his teeth with *khell*, which is the hard stamen of a plant which is also used in the preparation of a medicine for kidney disease. In this home herbal treatment, aids to beauty are not lacking: for removing freckles you will be offered a tincture called *gawi*, made from tree-resin, and for hair beauty every Egyptian knows the value of henna, castor oil and quinine. But the most widely used of all herbs is *helba*, justly described as the "queen of medicines," whose beneficial qualities are said to penetrate every living tissue of the body.

Much as health and beauty lie in perfection of face and figure, they lie also in grace of movement. Not only is it the Egyptian agricultural worker who, by the very nature of his toil, is graceful: the people as a whole have for generations considered suppleness as a pre-requisite to beauty. There are many different means of achieving this end, not the least of which perhaps being regular massage and manipulation of the joints, and the modern chiropractor has realized the necessity of supple joints for general health and has developed the practice on scientific lines. Here again, the Egyptian long ago forestalled the practitioner of today, and for many generations has been using the self-same methods for creating a healthy and graceful body. Writing over a hundred years ago, Lane described the routine at the public baths as follows:

> The bather sits on a marble seat ... or by the edge of one of the tanks to submit to the first operation, which is that of cracking his joints. The operator cracks almost every joint of his frame: he wrings the body, first one way, and then the other, to make several of the vertebrae crack; even the neck is made to crack twice, by wrenching the head round, each way, which produces a sensation rather alarming to an inexperienced person; and each ear is generally twisted round until it cracks: the limbs are wrested with apparent violence; but with such skill, that an untoward accident in this operation is never heard of. The main object of this process is to render the joints supple.

Incidentally, we do not recommend the uninitiated to try this performance on their own!

Religion also plays a big part in the attainment of suppleness. Devotions are one of the "cornerstones" of Islam, demanding the prostration of the body in several different positions at five prayer times daily. Such devotions—quite apart from their spiritual value—afford the devotee the benefit of what amounts to nearly one hour's rhythmical exercise each day—a factor not to be discounted in any health scheme.

From every point of view it must be agreed that Egypt throughout the centuries has made a great contribution to world knowledge in the search for health and beauty. The pursuance of the ideal has been and continues to be an unending struggle against man's enemy, disease. Though the ideal still in many cases continues to elude the seeker, yet armed with her rich heritage modern Egypt looks forward with confidence to the future.

Egyptian Radio, 1950

****

Some people eat dates,
whereas others get pelted with date stones.

****

The Street Vendors of Cairo

El weda' ya burto'an! "Farewell O oranges!" The sad cry of the orange-seller reminds us once again that winter is over—ahead lie the months of sand-storm and heat. But more than that, it reminds us what an important part in the life of the country is played by these itinerant vendors and how their songs and the wares they eulogize establish, as faithfully as do the calendar and clock, not only the changing seasons but also the passing hour. They are as integral a part of the Egyptian scene as the Nile and the palm trees.

There are, I believe, parts of Cairo where these vendors are debarred from hawking their wares. It seems to me a pity that this should be so because thereby the inhabitants are deprived not only of much that is picturesque and colourful in the country, but also an understanding of the people themselves—their character and humour.

From early in the day until late at night the vendors and their songs are with us. The peasant women with their cries of "morning milk" and "fresh eggs" are the first to break the hush of early morning. At night in the summer it is the seller of gherkins who sings our lullaby: in the winter the hawker of roasted nuts. Throughout the day comes a continuous stream of vendors, offering wares of every description: beans and cheese for the breakfast table; all kinds of vegetables and fruits; *gaz* or paraffin with which to cook the day's main meal; baskets, carpets, tin household utensils, feather and palm-fibre brooms, loofahs for the bath, and so on. The majority of these sellers come in the morning, providing material for the day's housework and preparation of the large mid-day meal. An then, when work is over and luncheon eaten and enjoyed, comes the mournful cry of one who repairs primus stoves, on which the greater part of the cooking is done. Is it because of the joyless nature of his task that his call is so plaintive, or his realization of the moral implied: after the feast comes the reckoning?

It is not only the primus stove repairer who sings in this minor key. The mender of chairs, the locksmith and the ambulant plumber also intone in the same dreary manner, and sometimes I wonder whether perhaps there is a college for street vendors, divided up into the various faculties, where each trade may learn the song or dirge of his respective merchandise! Perhaps there are codes of professional etiquette that govern the nature of the song and prevent the infringement on the rights of one group by members of another? There certainly seems to be some kind of gentlemen's agreement between individual vendors that one should be permitted to finish his call before the other begins. This is surely as much a matter of good salesmanship as good manners, because the noise and confusion caused when two sellers find themselves chanting at the same time has to be heard to be believed. What is, however, more probable than a school for street vendors is that trading in one or other form of merchandise is a family affair, handed on from father to son, and thus the elements of the song remain the same, varying only in accordance with the artistic abilities of the vendors.

Though the songs of the various hawkers each have their particular charm, it is the vendors of fruits, vegetables and other eatables whose eulogies are the most interesting and picturesque.

It is obviously more easy to wax sentimental over a bunch of grapes than a feather broom, and the ways in which these vendors describe their wares seem often to indicate a genuine personal love for the article concerned. In the language of today, I suppose many of them would be termed symbolists, as often they refer to their goods with words which create an image in the mind of the hearer, rather than using those expressions more commonly employed. For example, the tomato-seller cries: *Rommaan, 'al ya 'oota,"* "pomegranates, O beautiful tomatoes" or *"gawaher, 'al ya 'oota,"* "jewels, O fine tomatoes!" The gherkin seller, in referring to his wares, likens them to *lubia,* or runner beans—they presumably being one of the most tender of vegetables in his opinion. In some cases, the goods for sale are only alluded to, without their actual name ever being mentioned: *"Wala teen, wala 'enab zayyak."* "Neither figs nor grapes are like you!" The season of the latter is past, and their delights enjoyed; then comes the date, which is thus described as being even more delicious—in a class by itself in fact. Neither does the vendor of *laban zabadi,* or yoghourt, refer to his product by name, but his cry is full of the wisdom of the East:

"Errak 'ala es san'a ya laban, ya 'eshta." ("It all depends on the art of making. O milk, O cream.")

The apricot, or *mish-mish,* has a whole verse in its praise:

"Elli estawa, we taab, we talab el akkal, Ya Hamawi, ya na'em." ("That which has ripened, become good, and asked for the eater. Oh smooth *Hamawi." Hamawi* being a species of apricot.) Sometimes, too it is described as "pink-cheeked, smooth *Hamawi."*

The verse by which *malana,* or split-peas, are offered for sale is particularly charming:

El malana lawwezet, we el 'azba etgawwezet, el arageen ya malana. ("The *malana* have become like almonds, and the spinster has married, O beautiful spray of *malana.*")

Batikh—or water-melon—is offered "on the knife": in other words, the buyer is invited to cut the fruit to test its excellence. The seller of shammaam, or sugar melon, goes one better and offers his wares "on the pen-knife," thereby implying the greater delicacy and refinement of this fruit. Some things are so excellent in themselves and their virtues so apparent as to require no adjectives of praise. Such is the case with strawberries and grapes, which are only referred to by their varying species. *Melokheyya*—vegetable most beloved by all Egyptians—needs nothing but its name to commend it!

While undoubtedly the food vendors are the most melodious and their cries the most interesting, yet others also have their appeal to the eye or to the ear. One of the most attractive of these is the seller of *'olla,* or clay jugs, which are used for cooling drinking-water. As he pushes along his loaded cart, he beats out a fascinating oriental rhythm on his *darabukka,* or peasant drum. This is the instrument which accompanies most Egyptian dancing, and the sense of rhythm is so strong in these people that even tiny children will strum out a few beats on the *darabukka* as early as they learn to talk. And then there is the flute-vendor, piping out a little ditty to advertise his wares, and the feather-broom seller with his long bamboo-handled brooms reaching skywards, as though to brush away the clouds. A very colourful picture is the basket-seller as he comes swaying down the road—himself a pyramid consisting of every conceivable variety and colour of wicker-work receptacle. How he manages to load up his wares in the first place and, having once set them down to trade, pile them up again on his person, is a continual source of wonder. A note from the *Thousand and One Nights* is provided by the modern Aladdin who offers *Saxonia,* or fine quality china goods, in exchange for old clothes and household objects. And last but not least in this parade comes the *sharbat,* or sweet-drink seller who, with his gaily striped apron and his long-spouted vessel strapped to his side, announces his approach by a merry little castanet rhythm on his metal cups.

No doubt many of the vendors of the past have gone and new ones taken their place. The greater part of those whom Edward Lane mentions in his book—published over a hundred years ago—no longer grace the streets of Cairo; instead, we hear the more modern cry of "ice cream" from the tricycle-rider—this latter being very modern, as the confection now called ice cream went until recently by the Turkish name *kaimak,* the Italian *gelati,* or the Turkish *dundorma.* Another modern word the vendors have added to their vocabulary is "nylon"—since that material of many uses and forms appeared out of the West. Ties, watches, sun-glasses, socks, balloons—and even fish—to name only a few—are referred to as *"Ya nylon!"*

But while the old order has changed in some respects, the

95

main body of vendors remains the same, and by their coming and going and the varying goods they offer for sale we are able to check the season as it advances. The passing of the orange and other citrus fruits marks the end of winter; with *Shem el Neseem,* the spring feast, the *malana* season is over and from then onwards the summer fruits follow each other in regular succession. So clearly do the fruits and vegetables mark the passing year that people will offer each other the traditional greeting: *"kol sana w' enta tayyeb"*—"may every year find you well"—with the arrival of one or the passing of another. And when the fruits of summer are over, the Nile has flooded and brought its rich life-giving deposits for the new season's crops, when the first mists of autumn rise from the river—it is the cry of a street vendor that heralds the approaching winter: *El rommaan yefakkar el 'aryan,* "The pomegranate warns the naked one."

Egyptian Radio, 1948

***

Go with the liar until the door of the house.

***

Buskers and Street-Vendors of Cairo and London

Street-vendors and buskers seem to be very much in the news these days: various London street associations have even gone so far as to complain to the Home Secretary about the nuisance caused by unlicensed street traders, while the buskers haunting the rabbit-warrens of London's Underground, regaling the hurrying crowds with a tune on the guitar, have been dispatched with scant ceremony, warned that their behaviour is illegal. At the same time a well-known national newspaper has pasted up a number of rather attractive pictures of street-vendors of old, such as the knife-grinder, the buyer of rabbit-skins, and the like, with the comment that the viewer—you or I—could get a better job than this if we scanned the columns of this particular newspaper!

I have always been fascinated by street-vendors—even scared stiff of them! I remember very well as a small child feeling my hair stand on end when I heard the mournful cry of the old-clothes man down our street. It was my grand-parents' house, and I recall pulling back the lace curtains ever so slightly to catch a glimpse of the man as he passed—but making sure he didn't see me! "Any old clothes to sell?" he intoned, and somehow I had an awful feeling that if he saw me he would whisk me into his sack and that would be the end of me! In those days, the old-clothes man was a poor enough fellow, walking the quiet streets with his sack slung over his shoulder: his counterpart of today is much more prosperous-looking, with his cart and well-fed horse, but maybe he inspires the same fear in some other childish breast! Anyhow, he is one of the few remaining street-vendors or buskers around London these days, and for that reason I suppose I should be sorry if he disappeared for good, like most of his ilk.

When I went to live in Egypt I found myself charmed and attracted by the street vendors and buskers, just as the English writer Edward Lane had been over a century previously. Certainly, the old-clothes man was there too, but with a difference! Like the seller of lamps in *Aladdin,* this one offered new china-ware in exchange for old clothes or household articles, so of course I felt myself transported back into the atmosphere of *The Thousand and one Nights,* and not frightened as I had been as a child. At the Feast of the Pilgrimage we see him around too: this time he is buying skins, like the man in the newspaper advertisement I mentioned earlier: but he is not buying rabbit skins, but sheep skins, stripped from the sheep slaughtered on the first day of the Feast of the Sacrifice, commemorating Abraham's sacrifice of a sheep in place of his son. We hear him early in the morning, just after the Dawn Prayer, but I doubt the particular tone of his cry inspires the kind of fear in a child's heart that I felt years ago.

In the old English folk-song, the vendor is calling out: "chairs to mend, old chairs to mend!" but I have not caught sight of this street-crier in London for many a long year. In Cairo, though, he is still around, and makes a very good job of mending the seats of old "rush or cane-bottomed" chairs. His friend the seller of baskets is one of the most colourful of Cairene vendors. It's always a wonder to me how he manages to pile up his collection of baskets on his person and then come swaying down the road, looking like a wicker-work pyramid. I think he must be a relation of the Covent

Garden traders who compete to see who can carry the most fruit baskets on their heads!

It is quite a surprise to find that the knife-grinder is still to be seen in the streets of London, though he is not a frequent passer, and of course never appears when one needs him! In spite of modern technological advance, however, he is still needed, and there are always knives, scissors or shears to be sharpened: and how convenient it is to have it done on the spot! We have him still in Cairo, and the strange thing is that the one who comes down our street looks just like the one of the newspaper adverstisement I mentioned. Knife-grinding must attract similar types, wherever they are.

Another vendor I remember as a child was the muffin-man. He used to walk along the street with his wares on a tray on his head, ringing a bell to attract customers. Buying muffins from him on a Sunday afternoon was one of the pleasures of my childhood, and I was very pleased to find plenty of vendors like him when I went to Cairo. In fact, most of them carry their goods on their heads, though they do not ring a bell like the muffin-man; instead, they have their little songs to advertise what they are selling, and sometimes they wax quite poetical over them.

Just as the street-criers of London have attracted artists over the years, and have found their way into folk-song and opera, and have been painted and reproduced on such every-day articles as table-mats and even jig-saw puzzles, so have those of Cairo been reproduced in folk-dance and ceramics. Years ago, when I first went to Egypt, the street-vendors and their cries were just considered a nuisance; but more recently, their particular artistic merit has been appreciated and they are being "potted" in one way or another before they, too, disappear like their London counterparts.

I have been disappointed to find that the London busker entertaining theatre queues is almost a thing of the past: of course, there are no more queues for balcony seats like there used to be, and the London busker is hard put to it to find a replacement for this audience. Then, too, many buskers have made their way into television, and here again, the situation is the same in Egypt. There are still flame-swallowers, acrobats and conjurers producing chicks from under basins—the old *gulla-gulla* men of Port Said who delighted the passengers from ocean liners passing through the

Suez Canal: but most of these find it far more profitable to perform at children's birthday parties, or if they are lucky, to get a contract on TV. There are still Punch and Judy shows in the streets on feast days, like those at seaside resorts in Britain: in fact, this particular busker performance seems most likely of all to endure. As yet, we have not got any busking guitarists in Cairo: but there is a seller of bamboo flutes, also to be seen around the streets on feast days, followed Pied-Piper-wise by the children as he plays his little tune.

Yes, I shall be sorry to see the end of the street-vendors and buskers, in Cairo as well as in London. Even if, like the old-clothes man of my childhood, they do chill my bones, I still find them one of the more colourful aspects of life.

Radio London, 1972

***

If you marry a monkey for his money,
his money will disappear and the monkey remain.

***

The Old Folks of Egypt

Old people in Egypt are seldom lonely. It is very rare indeed to find an elderly person living on his or her own: old folks have a place in the family. A father may live with his son or daughter, but it is the custom for a mother to live with her son—her eldest son. This may be rather hard on the daughter-in-law, but no doubt she draws comfort from the knowledge that her day will come—that is, if she has sons—and that she will have her rightful place one day in the home of her son. And so it goes on. The old grandmother has her uses, of course: the most important of these is looking after the grandchildren, and so Grandma (*Setti* or "My Lady") is kept pretty busy looking after the children while Mum goes out to work. But things are moving fast now in this timeless land. Women of the last generation or two are educated, often highly educated, and they hold on to their jobs after marriage. Moreover, the educated woman of today will not necessarily be content to live with her children when she grows old and is widowed; she may want to keep her independence, and will most likely have earned a pension that will enable her to do so.

But even in the past, there were some independent spirits who disliked the idea of hitching their wagon to that of one of their children. It was not that they felt it was wrong for the children to be saddled with an aged parent: they wanted to retain their own individuality, not to have it submerged in that of their son's or daughter's. My husband's grandmother was such a one. She was over ninety when I first came to Egypt. She was practically bedridden by then, but she insisted on living on her own with one faithful retainer, to whom she used to call out her orders, as though to the houseful of servants she had had when young. She was certainly an autocratic old lady. She never left the house—she had not done so for years—but sat in state in her bedroom and received members of the family in queenly audience. When old age claimed her teeth, she resolutely refused to wear dentures. She took one look at the set when they arrived from the dentist and put them away in the cupboard, where they remained to her dying day. Not for her was the complaint that we are "slaves to our teeth." She managed very well indeed without hers!

But Egyptians are very conservative: they have so many thousands of years of history behind them, and many of the customs go right back to Pharaonic times. An Egyptologist friend told me that as far back as the Old Kingdom (that is about 3,000 B.C.) there are references to the position of elderly people in the family, and we see how greatly they were revered. So about 5,000 years ago, the Vizier Ptah-Hotep gave some "Instructions on Wisdom" to his son, just as Polonius did. He gave him the do's and don'ts of correct behaviour, and he called his son the "prop" of his old age. A son, he said, should take care of his mother and never disobey her. The ideal family set-up then was for the whole family to be living together, with the old people giving advice, and telling tales to their grand-children in the evening. The greatest joy was for the grandfather to see his own children carrying on his work when old age made this impossible for him.

This picture of the united family is carried on into present-day Egypt, governed by the ideals of religion. The words of the Qor'an rule the way of life of the people—consciously or unconsciously—and in the Qor'an children are exhorted to respect and honour their parents, and reminded to take care of their mother, never say a harsh word against her or complain about her. "Paradise lies at the feet of mothers" is a saying of the Prophet Mohammed.

It is always difficult to generalize about anything in Egypt, because there is such a difference between the rural and urban population. But there are certain common factors, and I think that respect of the young for their elders is one. A daughter will kiss her mother's hand as a matter of course, and I've known a man in his thirties—a hardened smoker of forty cigarettes a day, and with nicotine-stained fingers—refraining from smoking in front of his father, although his father knew he smoked, and he knew his father knew—and so on.

Egyptians have plenty of respect for elderly people, but they do not mind having a joke or two at their expense. Nobody can resist the spectacle of a group of old women gossiping away—at feast time, at births and weddings. "If there were a marriage in heaven, the old women would put up a ladder in the sky," the saying goes.

And what about elderly people in retirement? I suppose they are much the same as elsewhere. Some have their hobbies—reading, chess, dominoes, tric-trac—and talking! The Egyptians of any age are great talkers, and most of all they like to meet their friends in clubs and cafés. This is true of townsman and villager alike. The little sidewalk cafés are the haunt of retired men, morning and afternoon—rather like English pubs—and here the older ones meet to read the newspapers and discuss politics and family affairs. And if there has been a death in their midst—a relative, friend or acquaintance—they will be performing the duty of walking in the funeral procession and attending the sober evening wake, paying their last respects and offering condolences.

I think in many ways old people in Egypt come into their own when they grow old and retire. Even if they do not live with their families, they are surrounded by them and never left to be lonely. I remember my old father-in-law. He was a retired judge, and was completely blind for the last few years of his life. But as the eldest male member of the family he was held in high esteem and enjoyed the greatest respect of the other members of the family. He used to sit in his room, receiving visitors and dispensing advice all day long. That was still in the days of the "landed gentry" in Egypt, and because of his senior status, he was responsible for receiving the income from the land and distributing it. So everyone came to him—for advice, to arrange loans, to discuss ways of planting the land and increasing their income. Those days all belong to the past: the old man is long since dead and gone, and there are no more landed gentry in Egypt. But the old traditions of courtesy and respect remain, and I doubt they will ever disappear from this ancient land.

B.B.C. "Home This Afternoon", 1966

***

*If you teach your little child good behaviour,
you will be happy with him when he grows up.*

***

Tales for the Young in Arabic Literature

The Arabic-speaking child is perhaps fortunate in having available in his own language the colourful stories which make up the *Thousand and One Nights:* indeed, of these, the "Adventures of Sinbad" still remains one of the most popular tales of adventure. But there are many others to be had in Arabic besides the *Arabian Nights,* and in these stories we meet knights errant, we hear of battles fought for love of fair ladies and for vengeance, and of strange adventures on desert isles, such as delight the heart of any child in any land. And in addition to these tales of Arabic origin, there is a large amount of material translated from other languages, and so the Arabic-speaking child can get to know about such legendary figures as Robin Hood, Gulliver and Robinson Crusoe.

When he first comes across *Robinson Crusoe,* the Arabic-speaking schoolboy may quite likely be struck by the resemblance between Daniel Defoe's famous novel and the story written by an Arabic scholar, Ibn Tofayl, a doctor and writer of Granada who lived in Moslem Spain some five hundred years before the birth of Daniel Defoe. Ibn Tofayl's story tells of *Hyy, ibn Yaqzan*—"Alive, Son of Aware"—who was cast adrift into the sea as an infant and washed up on a desert island, where he grew to manhood with only the birds and animals of the isle for his companions.

There is an obvious similarity between the two narratives, though the tales differ in that Robinson Crusoe was a grown man when he was shipwrecked, whereas Hyy ibn Yaqzan was a tiny child, and all that he could know of life he learnt from the creatures of the island, and not from any human being. In Ibn Tofayl's tale (which was translated into English "to be read by the Quakers amongst books of piety," as mentioned by Ahmed Amin in the introduction to his book in which he edited three different stories about Hyy Ibn Yaqzan) the hero lives a life of solitude until one day he encounters a stranger from the race of men, who has fled from his island home nearby. The stranger explains to Hyy about the world from which he comes, of the language, religions and customs of the people, and together they visit the stranger's inhabited island. However, they soon come to realize that their life of solitude is preferable, and return to the desert island of Hyy, there to resume the life which Hyy had been pursuing, a life of observation and reflection.

One of the most colourful figures in Arabic literature is *'Antarah ibn Shaddad* (sometimes known as *Abul Fawaris*—"Father of the Knights"). The life and adventures of this pre-Islamic warrior-poet have provided rich material for books and plays, and to most Arabic-speaking children 'Antarah represents their ideal of chivalry and valour. The story of 'Antarah is a romantic one: though his father was one of the chiefs of his tribe, his mother was a slave-girl, and 'Antarah was therefore not considered an equal with the freemen of the tribe. However, 'Antarah was soon able to force his personality on his tribe, and to gain an undisputed place among the tribal leaders. In fact, he was to prove to be the bravest and the most eloquent, becoming known throughout the Arabian Peninsula for both his courage and his poetry, in which he spoke with typical Arab pride of his own daring exploits, of the excellence of his tribe, and of his love for his cousin 'Ablah.

The romance of *'Antarah*, added to by every passing generation, has been handed on down the years, and sung by the minstrel up to this day in town and village, providing rich material for modern novelists and playwrights. The great Egyptian poet of modern times, Ahmed Shawky, wove one of his verse-dramas around the romantic figure of 'Antarah, while Mahmud Teymur deals with the same theme in his play *Eternal Eve,* where he concentrates on the relationship between 'Antarah and 'Ablah. Truly, the story of 'Antarah is one which will continue to stir the imagination of all who delight in tales of courage and adventure.

The story of *Abu Zeid el Hilaly* (an interpretation of which was staged recently in Cairo) is another which has been told down the years by the minstrel in Egypt. Accompanied on the *rababa* (a one-stringed instrument), the village bard sings of the exploits of this hero in Egypt and North Africa round about the 11th century. As in the case of 'Antarah, the hero has become a legendary figure, and the story of his adventurous life and his deeds of daring have enchanted countless generations.

Arabic-speaking children can certainly find a wealth of adventure and travel tales in their native language, thrilling their minds and firing their imaginations, and at the same time presenting for them ideals of courage, endurance and leadership.

The Egyptian Gazette, February, 1979

***

The morning greeting of a monkey is better than that of a moustacheless man.

***

Mother's Day in Egypt

Mother's Day is celebrated in Egypt on the 21st of the beautiful month of March. The tradition was introduced into this country by the late 'Ali Amin, co-founder of *Akhbar El Yom* newspaper, some years ago. However, there is little doubt that a similar occasion must have been celebrated throughout the history of this country. Motherhood is held in very high esteem in Egypt and the Moslem world. One of the *hadeeth,* or sayings of the Prophet Mohammed, is: "Paradise lies at the feet of mothers." There is also a well-known saying in Arabic, *"al omm madrasatun,"* meaning the mother is a school. In fact, this reverence for mothers can be traced back to Pharaonic times. The Ancient Egyptians had various gods connected with motherhood, the first of whom being Isis, the wife of Osiris and mother of Horus, the hawk-headed god. Her chief names, as given in the *Book of the Dead,* translated by E.A. Wallis Budge, are the "great goddess," the "divine mother," and "mother of the gods." She is most commonly represented as the mother suckling her child Horus. Some particularly fine sculptures of her may be seen at the Ptolemaic temple of Horus at Edfu, between Luxor and Aswan. Hathor, the cow-goddess, was also associated with motherhood. She was known as the giver of life and protectress of mothers. Her temple, also of Ptolemaic date, is at Denderah, in the same area as Horus's temple. Ta-urt (Thoueris of the Greeks) was the hippopotamus goddess, protector of mothers during childbirth. Ta-urt was helped by the dwarf deity Bes, and the mother in labour would have statues or figurines of both goddesses in her birth chamber as wall decorations, which may be seen in Luxor temple.

With this long history of reverence for motherhood, it is natural that mothers are still held in high esteem in modern Egypt. Every year on this occasion an "ideal mother" is chosen for an extraordinary achievement for her family and is honoured by the government. And for this day, children buy presents for their mothers, to express their love and appreciation for the one who gave them life and cared for them from the day they were born. At school, children draw or paint a card, or perhaps fashion a gift for the day, and then in the morning thrust a bouquet of spring flowers into the hands of mothers.

Cairo Today, March, 1982

***

The one on the bank knows how to swim.

Our Bawab (Doorkeeper)

Two sounds clearly distinguish the bawab of our apartment building in Zamalek. One is the peaceful swish of his broom in the early morning as he sweeps the pathway below our bedroom window. The other is the great yawn he gives on a Thursday afternoon to herald the weekend. When recently he deserted his post for a week or so because of some disagreement with the landlord, we realized just how important a person the bawab is in Egyptian life.

The job of the bawab is to take care of the building. He is supposed to keep it clean, guard it, and deal with the various callers. During the day, when not working, he sits on a chair or wooden bench just outside or inside the building. At night, he sleeps in a little room near the entrance. In this way, he is able to keep check of anybody entering the building and to turn away any intruders.

Many of the bawabs come from Nubia and Aswan in Upper Egypt. They usually leave their families in their home towns or

106

villages, visiting them two or three times a year, at feast time or for a wedding, birth or death in the family. The rest of the time, they are attached to their building in Lower Egypt, in Cairo or Alexandria. Our bawab is not like these: he is from Upper Egypt, it is true, but not from Nubia or Aswan, and his skin is light, not black and shiny like that of the Nubians. His family is here in Cairo: not with him in the building, as with some bawabs, but in the town, and our bawab goes home most nights. He is able to do this as there is another bawab, much younger than ours, to share his duties: this one is true to type and sleeps in the building, going to his home in Aswan rarely—as recently, when he got married and went off for a month on his honeymoon: then he left his new bride to return to his post here in Zamalek.

Our bawab really does not need to work now, he assures us. His family is grown up and his sons are doing well in business. They would like their father to give up his job as bawab and they are more than ready to support him for the rest of his days, as is the custom in Egypt. But our bawab enjoys his job, and it is probably better for him than staying at home with nothing to do and getting in people's way. He leaves home early in the morning, arriving here at around 7 a.m. with the morning papers. His voice, with its cheerful *"Sabah el kheir"*—"Good Morning"—is a pleasant and reassuring sound, and is echoed by the other bawabs in the street with a greeting which goes one better, as in the custom, such as *"Sabah el 'eshta,"* "Morning of cream," or *"Sabah el ful"*—"Morning of jasmine."

Bawabs are part of the life of the building and the vicinity, and enter into the spirit and mood of whatever is going on. They will run small errands for the tenants, bargain for them with street vendors, and perhaps dust their cars, provided it does not interfere with their main task. During Ramadan afternoons, as the long day wears on and as the sunset hour approaches, they will sit listening to the Qor'an chanting on the radio, and on Ramadan evenings, after the fast is over, they sit at the entrance to the building, chatting with friends or other bawabs and listening to the special programmes of the month on their transistor radios. At feast time, they will be dressed in their best qaftans, greeting tenants and visitors with the traditional "May every year find you well." Our bawab is no exception to this: the first day of the feast he is there is full splendour in his new regalia, and it is not until the second or third day that he goes to celebrate at home.

According to the *Egyptian Gazette,* some people think that the system is out of date. They complain that bawabs do not do their jobs properly: some, they say, take on other jobs and leave their wives and children to look after the building, with the result that it is often dirty and unguarded. Such people suggest that it would be better to do away with the system and replace the bawab with an electronically-controlled iron gate and bell such as is found in some other countries. In reply to this, one would ask how the building would be kept clean, who would answer the queries of callers, who would run errands, bring the morning papers, bargain with vendors over the price of bunches of mint, sweet potatoes, corn-on-cob or prickly pears? It would be a sad day for me if our bawab were to decide to stay at home and leave us to our own devices.

Nevertheless, there may one of these days no longer be any choice in the matter, and bawabs may become a thing of the past. Already, the race is threatened by the march of progress. Our bawab can hardly read or write, but his children are educated and would certainly not take on the job of their father, as was often the case in the past. Education is free in Egypt now, and the sons of bawabs in our street have got university degrees or certificates from technical colleges, and many have gone to work in other Arab countries. So who is going to work as a bawab in future? Whatever one's feelings on the subject, therefore, the time does not seem far distant when a system other than that of the bawab will become inevitable. That is why I continue to be grateful for the presence of our bawab, despite his upsetting of the peace of the street sometimes with his loud and domineering voice. Long may we continue to hear his Thursday yawns and the swish of his broom in the early morning!

Written for *Nile Reflections,* 1984.

***

Find a husband for your daughter,
but don't find a bride for your son.

FOOD AND HOSPITALITY IN EGYPT

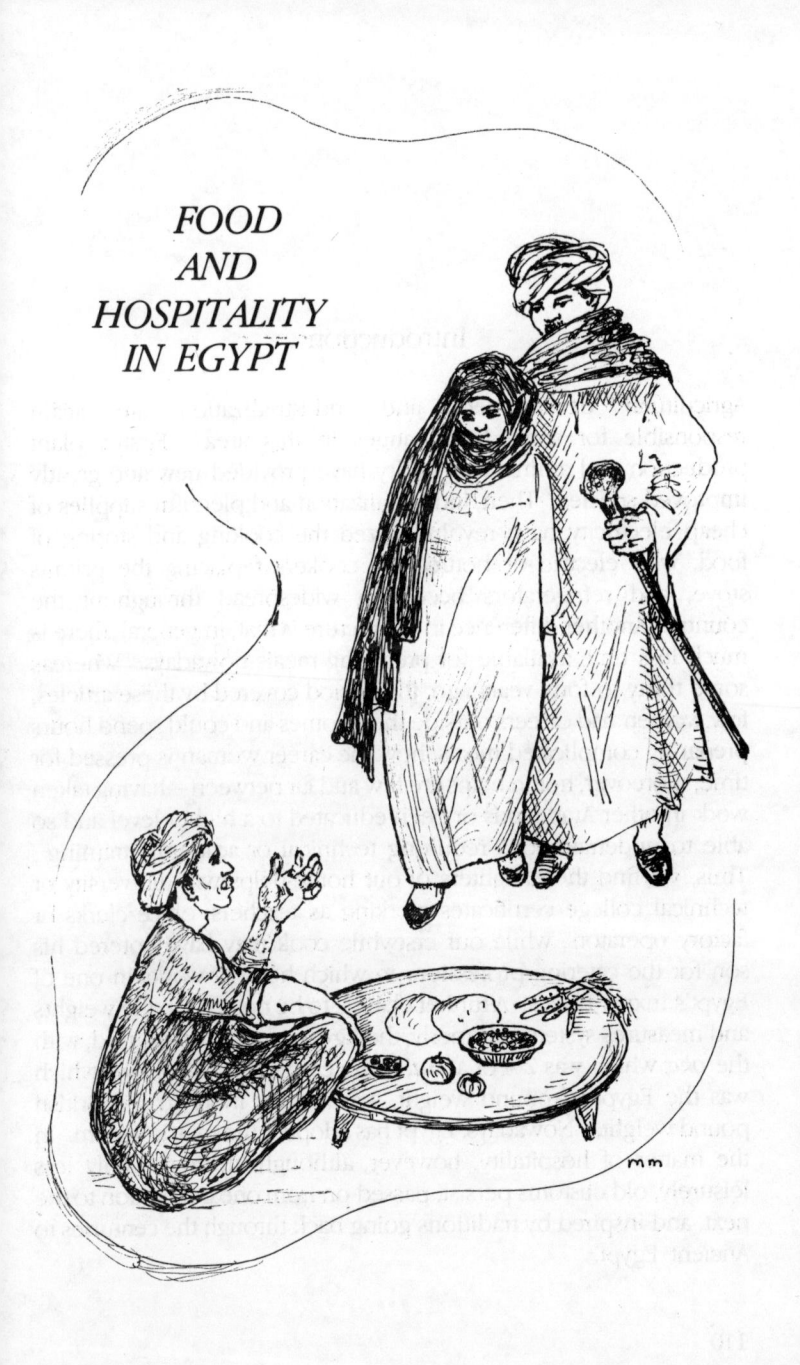

Introduction

Agricultural development and industrialization are again responsible for some big changes in this area. Firstly, plant production and animal husbandry have provided new and greatly improved species. Then, industrialization and plentiful supplies of cheap electricity have revolutionized the cooking and storing of food, with electric or bottled-gas cookers replacing the primus stove, and refrigerators becoming widespread throughout the country. Another difference in the picture is that, in general, there is much less time available for preparing meals nowadays. Whereas some thirty to forty years ago, the period covered by these articles, few women had careers outside their homes and could spend hours preparing complicated meals, now the career woman is pressed for time; moreover, home-helps are few and far between—having taken work in other Arab lands or been educated to a higher level and so able to undertake jobs requiring technical or academic training. Thus, we find the daughters of our home-helps with university or technical college certificates working as teachers, office clerks or factory operators, while our erstwhile cook may have entered his son for the catering profession, in which he now works in one of Egypt's luxury hotels! A further change to be noted is in the weights and measures systems: formerly, the Egyptian system was used, with the *oke,* which was 2¾ of a *rutl* being employed. (The *rutl,* which was the Egyptian pound weight, was slightly more than a British pound weight.) Nowadays, Egypt has adopted the metric system. In the matter of hospitality, however, although life is certainly less leisurely, old customs persist, passed on from one generation to the next, and inspired by traditions going back through the centuries to Ancient Egypt.

***

Egyptian Table Talk

The Egyptians have a proverb which says, "The clever one spins with a donkey's leg," and nowhere is this saying more appropriate than in regard to the culinary art in Egypt, if one considers the marvels produced from that most widely used article of cookery—the primus stove. It is, of course, all a question of attitude, and only in a country where cooking has been raised to the standard of an art, and eating regarded as one of the pleasures of life, could so much have been achieved with what today may be regarded as a rather primitive implement.

But let us distinguish quite clearly between a gourmet and a gourmand. The Egyptians themselves have something to say in this connection. Kaqemni, an Egyptian sage of ancient times, said: "Restrain thy appetite, for greediness savoureth of the beasts. The man who permitteth his appetite to guide him is an abomination." And the prophet Mohammed remarked: "We are a people who do not eat before we are hungry, and when we eat we do not satiate ourselves."

If the Egyptians have earned a reputation for their culinary art, they have an equally well-deserved reputation for hospitality, born of a desire to give of their utmost to their guest that he may share in the delights of the table and they in the pleasure of the company. The ideal of Arab generosity towards guests is personified in Hatim Tayyi, of whom many anecdotes are told. He lived in pre-Islamic days in Arabia, and his fame spread far beyond the borders of his own country, until it reached the ears of the Emperor of Byzantium at Constantinople. The Emperor was curious to find out whether this legendary generosity of Hatim Tayyi were indeed true. He sent an ambassador to Hatim to ask as a gift his mare—a fine thoroughbred well-known throughout Arabia for her speed and prowess in battle and in the hunt. On his arrival, he was treated with the generosity which had made Hatim Tayyi's name famous, and after the sumptuous repast the ambassador delivered himself of his mission. "My master, the Emperor of Byzantium, asks for your mare as a gift to grace his stables." But Hatim had already slaughtered his beloved mare to provide the meal for his guest. . . . She was all he had!

Hospitality has continued to be a feature of Arab life, and the Egyptian peasant, like Hatim Tayyi, will slaughter his last sheep for his guest. What there is, be it only a dish of beans, must be shared, and the passer-by will always be hailed and invited *"Etfuddal"*—"Pray join us." This attitude can, and in some cases does, lead to some humorous situations. The Nile boatmen, sitting around their meal as their feluka sails quietly upstream, will call to the passer-by on the banks "Pray join us." In most cases, naturally, this is an impossibility and the Egyptian calls any similar invitation *'ozoomet marakbeyya*—"boatman's invitation"—implying one of which it is well-nigh impossible to avail oneself.

In this matter of hospitality, the onus is not entirely on the host, and the guest will naturally play his part in making the occasion a gay and happy one. After the meal, there will be leisurely conversation over a cup of Turkish coffee, and here the Egyptians have a word for the uncivilized fellow who does not comply with the dictates of seemly behaviour. *El daif el magnoon yakol we ye'oom.* "The mad guest eats and goes away!"

There are many pleasantries exchanged in the course of eating and drinking. After the meal, the guest will say: *Sofra daima"*—"May your table be full always." To this, his host will reply: *"Allah yedoom 'ezzak"*—"May your prosperity remain for ever." When the guest has drunk his glass of water, he will be told: *"Haneyyan"*—"May it prove wholesome to you," to which his answer is: *"Allah yehanneek"*—"May God give you pleasure." There are other courtesies of this nature, not necessarily connected with the meal. The hostess will say to the departing guests: *"Anestoona"*—"You have cheered us and made us happy by your company." *"Allah ye'ansek,"* the guests reply. "May God be always your companion."

Although the Egyptians could in no way be described as vegetarians, yet they have mastered the art of cooking vegetables in many varied and delightful ways, and the vegetable dishes share pride of place with those consisting of meat. In Britain, if you were asked what you would like for the day's meal, your mind would immediately conjure up visions of fish, flesh or fowl! Here in Egypt, the enquiry and reply concern the vegetables, of which there are all the year round a vast variety from which to choose. The vegetables are cooked and presented in dozens of different ways; I was told there are no fewer than seventy ways of cooking aubergines alone! These ways, however, do not include boiling. The mere thought of boiled vegetables fills the average Egyptian with horror, as he associates this with sickness and invalid diet.

The Ancient Egyptians seem to have eaten very much the same foods as are eaten in Egypt today. A study of their paintings, texts and records, and the foodstuffs they mummified and had buried with them for use in their afterlife, can give us a good idea of the diet of the Ancient Egyptians. Apart from vegetables and fruits of all kinds, they ate the meat of cows, goats and gazelles. They were great sportsmen, and the prizes of the day's sport—such as pigeons, geese, and wild duck from the marshes—formed a large part of their cuisine, as well as fish from the river and lakes. The pig was apparently held in low esteem, according to Adolf Erman in *Life in Ancient Egypt*. This was possibly for religious reasons, and E.A. Wallis Budge in *The Dwellers on the Nile* says it was probably eaten by the "slaves and swamp dwellers."

The women of Ancient Egypt were very good housewives and excelled in the art of bread, biscuit and cake-making. They prepared their own jams and preserves from the plentiful fruits at their disposal and, like their sisters in present-day Egypt, made their own butter and *samna,* which they stored in earthenware jars. Islam forbids alcoholic drinks, but the Ancient Egyptians were masters in the art of making wines from grapes and dates, and *boozah*—a kind of ale—from barley, though warnings against excess in drinking were given by the sages, as Wallis Budge points out.

Egypt is part of the Islamic world and we therefore find on the Egyptian table dishes having their origin in other parts of that world. From the Caucasus we get *shircaseyya*—a delicious preparation from the stock of chicken and finely ground walnuts, made into a thick sauce and served surrounded with mounds of rice. From Syria comes *kobeyba,* made from meat, a specially prepared flour, pine kernels and spices. Turkey brings us *yalangi dolma*—vine-leaves stuffed with rice, mint and parsley and served with yoghourt.

There are many other delicacies—savoury and sweet—from the various parts of the Middle East, too numerous to mention here. But there is one national dish greatly enjoyed by Egyptians and offered to foreign visitors as being typically Egyptian. This is *melokheyya*, made from the finely chopped leaves of a vegetable closely resembling mint and prepared with the stock of rabbit or chicken. Fried garlic and spices are added just before serving.

And now, having savoured some of the delights of the Egyptian table and spent some pleasant minutes of companionship in a discussion of the culinary art, I will bid you "Good bye" and *"Sofra daima"*—"May your table be full always."

Egyptian Radio, 1948

***

If your friend is honey, don't eat him all up.

***

The Fruits of Egypt

The year has been remarkably good for fruit, with new varieties appearing and well-known ones developed in improved quality. Outstanding this year was the strawberry crop, whose season lasts from November till the end of May. Strawberries for Christmas is one of the luxuries of Egypt, but this year the appearance and flavour of this fruit amazed everybody. It seems that it is being developed on a large scale in the Canal city of Ismailia, which provides the sandy soil most suitable for its growth.

Another fruit that has been considerably developed over the past few years is the peach. This year, in particular, an exquisite new variety has appeared, small and beautiful and grown in Sinai. Anyone who has seen the peach orchards in blossom in Sinai will not be surprised to know that this delicious fruit is produced there. Other varieties of peach are available, too, in greater quantities than those from Sinai, which, apart from being pleasing eaten raw, may be made into compote or a fine conserve.

The Horticultural Department of the Ministry of Agriculture has been active over the past thirty or so years in developing types of fruit hitherto unknown in Egypt. Amongst these are plums and apples, previously only available imported. Now, thanks to the efforts of Egyptian horticulturalists, fruit lovers can find many varieties of these fruits on market stalls, golden and dark red plums, green cooking apples and rosy eating ones to satisfy every taste.

One of the greatest delights of Egypt is in fact the wealth of fruit that abounds throughout the year. Egypt enjoys a temperate Mediterranean climate, and in the rich soil of the Nile valley and on the fringes of the desert practically every type of fruit may be grown. Now in September it is just the beginning of autumn, but many of the fruits of summer will be on sale for another month or so, until the weather becomes colder. There are still grapes to be had—more rich in colour and flavour than earlier in the summer, golden, red, purple, and perfumed—while figs are perhaps sweeter and more luscious than ever. Meanwhile, the date-palms are laden with their rich burden, and the street vendor sings its praises in his own inimitable way: "Neither figs nor grapes are like you, O dates," he chants. Indeed, they are both delicious and nourishing, and some kinds may be made into an excellent conserve. Mangoes, too, are in season now, and this choice fruit is available in every size and colour from mid-July until the end of October at least. And there are some fruits which come only with autumn and which seem to herald the approach of winter: among these are guava, custard apples or "cream" fruit and pomegranates which, according to the song of the street vendors, "warn the naked one" that cooler weather is at hand.

After the fruits of autumn, the many kinds of citrus fruits begin to ripen. First come sweet lemons, tangerines and oranges to suit every taste—*sukkary* or sweet, *baladi*, "of the country," a type very suitable for juice, fine navel oranges and blood oranges. And, too, there is grapefruit in abundance from now and for most of the year, while the delicious Egyptian lime becomes plump and juicy at this time, providing quantities of vitamin C in the most palatable form. The lime sellers are an attractive feature of the Egyptian scene, apparently preferring this trade to any other—though the other be more profitable.

In early spring, the apricot orchards are in bloom, and one day in May the seller of *mish-mish* is heard chanting his song of praise for the fruit. The Egyptian apricot is sweet and delicious in its brief—all too brief—season. Brief, too is the season of the mulberry, which is prolific throughout Egypt and which comes in early summer in white, red and purple varieties.

With the coming of summer, the really choice fruits of Egypt ripen in the hot, dry sunshine. Perhaps the greatest joy of the Egyptian summer and autumn is the wonderful variety of grapes. The vineyards of the Rhine and Burgandy are justly famous, but the grapes of Egypt can bear comparison with those of any country. The vineyards of Egypt are those of Gianaclis near Alexandria, where red, white and rose wines are produced, bearing such picturesque names as "Nefertiti," "Cleopatra," "Cru des Ptolemees," and "Omar Khayyam." Visitors to Egypt can see paintings of the grape harvest on ancient tombs in Luxor and Saqqara, and will realize that the country has always been famed for this fruit, and indeed, for wine-making. In *Life in Ancient Egypt,* Erman says "at all times wine was a favourite beverage," and "vines were much grown throughout the country," while Wallis Budge in *The Dwellers on the Nile* comments that "the drinking of wine in Egypt is as old as dynastic civilization."

The Coptic month of Abib corresponds roughly to July, and this month, according to an old country saying, "ripens the grapes and figs." Egyptian figs remain in season from July until October, and are unbelievably sweet and succulent. Figs flourish in sandy soil, and some of the best varieties come from the coastal areas of 'Agami and Balteem on the Mediterranean coast, where the sand gleams a brilliant white in the sunshine.

Melons of every description come with the summer, some lasting until early autumn. First to appear are honey-dew and sugar melons; then follow the big round and oval water-melons, with their red, thirst-quenching flesh. Melons are, indeed, a leading specialty of Egypt, and new types are constantly being developed in some of the reclaimed land, such as Tahrir Province, west of the Delta, on the fringes of the desert. The pumpkin is also to be seen on the fruiterers' stalls at this time, and is made into a dessert known as *'Ara' Istanbuli* or pumpkin pie! During the summer months, too, the cactus produces its juicy fruit, and at many a street-corner there may be seen the seller of "prickly pears," skillfully peeling his wares without actually touching the fruit inside.

The visitor to Egypt will always be delighted with the fruits he finds here—some familiar, some new to his senses. Meanwhile, research is constantly being carried out to improve the quality of Egyptian products and new varieties grown in reclaimed lands. So, among his other souvenirs, the visitor will surely remember Egypt as a land of abundant and delicious fruits.

Cairo Today, September, 1982

***

One night and the morning will come.

***

Season of Dates

September corresponds to the month of Toot in the Coptic calendar, which, adapted from that of Ancient Egypt, has long been used to plan the agricultural round. This month, which is the first month of the Coptic year and is named after Thot, the ancient Egyptian god of wisdom, is known as *Rotub Toot,* or "Ripe Toot," and this is the time for the date harvest. Everywhere throughout the country the palm trees are heavy with their clusters—golden, red, black and orange—and soon the fruit shops will be stocked with the different varieties, and the street vendors will sing their praise in their own lyrical fashion.

The well-known Egyptian poet Ahmed Shawky called dates "fruit of the rich, food of the poor," and this aptly describes them. A bedouin or peasant can have a meal complete in protein and carbohydrate with a handful of dates, while a diner at a smart restaurant can enjoy an elegant and delicious dessert with a selection of the golden and black varieties. As with everything else, prices have risen steeply in recent years, but dates of one kind or another remain within the means of everybody.

First to appear and cheapest are *Ambat,* small, golden and lush. By day, these are sometimes sold on the pavement by peasant women, who smilingly weigh out their wares on hand-scales from a huge basket made from palm leaves. Sometimes they are to be found piled high with consummate skill on barrows in the market place, at night shining in the light of the vendor's paraffin lamp.

After *Amhat,* other kinds of dates follow rapidly: black *Ramli,* which, as their name suggests, grow best in the sandy soil near the desert, dark red *Zaghloul,* scrunchy like apples, and coming to market still on their yellow stalks, and reddish-black, round *Bent 'Aisha.* Then, towards the end of the season, come the succulent brown dates from the oasis of Siwa and the crisp orange-coloured *Samaani,* from which a delicious preserve can be made.

Samaani date jam should be made when these dates first come in. Later, when they ripen, they are excellent when eaten raw, but not suitable for jam-making. The dates must be washed and scraped and covered with water, then boiled until tender, when their colour becomes dark red. Next, the dates are removed from the liquid and their stones taken out. At this stage, they can either be cut into small pieces, or a skinned almond inserted in the place of the stone. It is generally agreed, also, that cloves give a rather delicate flavour to date jam, so a few may be added if desired.

The fruit is then returned to the liquid, in which sugar equal in weight to the original unstoned dates has been dissolved. The mixture is now brought to the boil and simmered. When the jam is nearly cooked, the juice of limes in the ratio of two *lamoon baladi* to a kilo of dates is added. This makes the jam syrupy in consistency, and after a little more boiling the mixture will set slightly when tested on a saucer.

Date jam, or syrup, used in days not long gone by to be offered to guests as a delicacy in much the same way as nowadays sweetmeats and chocolates are offered. Some of the dishes in which they were served were quite exquisite, making the jam appear even more appetizing when seen through them. Such a dish might consist of a wine-coloured glass bowl, fitted into a silver filigree stand. Around this outer container spoons were suspended, and in the centre of the glass bowl would be an inner bowl containing water. In this the guests would place the spoons after they had tasted the jam. Such refinements belong to a more leisured way of life than ours, but the splendid Egyptian dates remain, to delight the eye and satisfy the appetite.

Cairo Today, September, 1981

***

Old women at a wedding eat and find fault.

The Day of the Apricot

"Can I have my bicycle now?" the small boy asked his father in a recent cartoon in a local newspaper, which showed a child pointing to a barrow piled high with apricots. Obviously the father, weighed down by the usual burdens of home and family, must have promised his son a bicycle *"Bukra, fil mish mish,"*—"Tomorrow, in the day of the apricot." The father would have been telling his son, more or less, that there was 'nothing doing,' for tomorrow never comes.

What has this fruit, so prolific in Egypt, done to deserve such a reputation? Its exquisite blossom first appears in early February, taking the wild Amsheer winds with beauty, and making an elegant house decoration, with its pale pink flowers and delicate black branches. Then, after a week or two of reminding everybody that spring is not far away, it disappears, leaving us to face the cold blustery days without its cheering presence.

Is it because the apricot blossom fades so fast that the country saying has arisen, or does it refer to the fruit that some three months later appears, heralded by the loving song of the street vendor:

"That which has become ripe, and asks for the eater,
 O smooth, pink-cheeked Hamawayy apricots."

Perhaps, after all, it is the fruit that has earned for itself the reputation of fast fleetingness, for no sooner is it 'all over,' in the American-English meaning of that term, flooding the market for two or three brief weeks, than it disappears, answering the British-English understanding of the term as 'gone for ever'.

Anyhow, even if the blossom and fruit are so elusive, we can at least preserve the latter, which, as though making up for being so short-lived in its fresh state, can be very easily turned into a superb jam. Any apricots will do, no matter what size, provided they are sound. In fact, those sold on barrows in the local markets, even more 'pink-cheeked' under the light of a guttering lamp, are probably more suitable and certainly cheaper than the large and luscious variety arranged so invitingly at the fruit shop.

The secret of apricot jam lies in the minimal amount of water needed, for once the fruit is stoned, weighed and washed and an equal quantity of sugar added, the juice begins to flow, and a pint of water will be quite sufficient for three kilos of apricots. The pan is then put on the flame and the sugar allowed to dissolve slowly. Meanwhile, about a dozen kernels of the apricot stones can be blanched and chopped, to be added to the cooking fruit. The juice of three limes should also be added when the sugar has dissolved. Then the mixture should be brought to the boil and allowed to cook briskly for about half-an-hour, stirred regularly with a wooden spoon to prevent the jam sticking to the pan.

When cool, the jam should be bottled in sterilized jars, when it will no doubt be relished by family and friends long after the smooth, pink-cheeked Hamaway has disappeared.

The Egyptian Gazette, May, 1981

***

If I beat my son, I like someone to stop me.

***

Food for the Fast and Feast

It must seem rather incongruous to be talking about food for the fast, when doing without food from dawn to sunset is the whole point of the month of Ramadan. In answer to this entirely reasonable criticism, let it be said that, in the first place, the faster has to eat when the sunset hour comes, and special foods are prepared for his "break-fast," or *iftar*.

Certainly one of the most welcome sights for the faster when he sits down to his sunset meal must be a brimming jug of *qamar-el-din,* "moon of religion," a delicious and nourishing drink made from sheets of dried apricots. The visitor or newcomer to Egypt must often wonder how those packets of folded orange cardboard-like substance he sees in the grocer's shop undergo a metamorphosis into the apricot drink he may be offered at an *iftar,* and may be surprised to learn how simple and painless is the transformation.

The sheets of dried apricots must be broken up into small pieces and covered with boiling water. This should be left to soak for a few hours, and then pressed through a sieve. After this, it is just a matter of adding as much or as little additional water and sugar as may be desired, according to individual taste.

A rather unusual blancmange may be made with *qamar-el-din*. In this case, a few spoonsful of cornflour starch should be dissolved in cold water, and the sweetened *qamar-el-din* liquid boiled and stirred into the starch. The mixture is then returned to the fire and boiled gently for ten minutes or so, stirred all the time. When cooked, the blancmange is poured into dishes, left to cool, and then decorated with sultanas and chopped nuts.

Two points may be borne in mind here. One is that an Egyptian housewife will seldom tell you exactly how much of a particular commodity should be employed, or exactly how long it should be cooked. She relies on her own judgment in these matters and the visitor to Egypt, after she gets over her initial panic at being left to her own devices, without the comforting proximity of a cookery-book, will find that her culinary efforts are altogether more attractive and tasty.

Secondly, don't just ask for "cornflour" in a grocer's shop where the different habits and customs of newcomers to the country many not be known. Ask for "cornflour starch," or "cooking starch," otherwise you'll find yourself with an oke of maize flour on your hands—which, by the way, makes excellent cakes but is not much use for blancmange.

And now you may like to know more about the two sweetmeats that are eaten during Ramadan—namely, *kunafa* and *qatayef*. Most people in Egypt will, at one time or another, have heard the cry of the street-vendor who sells these commodities in their raw state, and perhaps wondered what strange wares lay concealed in the round tray which the vendor balances on his head. *Kunafa*, uncooked, looks rather like vermicelli, and cooked, like shredded wheat, while *qatayef* looks like crumpets until stuffed and cooked.

Both sweetmeats are very easy to make, and both rely for their success on a good syrup, so that is the first thing to know how to make. For this, one cup of sugar and two cups of water should be boiled until the mixture becomes syrupy; then the juice of half a lime is added and, if desired, a few drops of vanilla or rose-water to give a distinctive flavour.

For *kunafa,* two pounds of the vermicelli-like substance are required, and half-a-pound of clarified butter (or substitute). The butter must be rubbed into the *kunafa,* and half this mixture placed in a greased oven-pan. Over this mixture should be spread a layer of chopped nuts and sultanas, and the remainder of the *kunafa* arranged over it. A little clarified butter is then dotted on top, and the sweet is baked in a very moderate oven until golden-brown. Sometimes not all the clarified butter is absorbed during cooking and, so that the sweet may not be too heavy, this surplus can be strained off when the *kunafa* comes out of the oven. Finally, the *kunafa* is turned out onto a serving-dish, and some of the prepared syrup poured over it. But make sure the syrup is cold, otherwise it may make the *kunafa* doughy.

Even easier to make is *qatayef*. All that is required is to stuff the crumpet-like objects with chopped nuts and sultanas, fold them over and press the edges together to make them stick, and then fry in boiling clarified butter until pale gold in colour. Immediately on removal from the pan, the *qatayef* should be dropped into a bowl of the prepared syrup, and left to soak in this for a few minutes and then placed on a serving-dish.

Both these sweetmeats are distinctly on the rich side, but they are delicious and make a welcome addition to the dinner-table at any time of the year.

And now we come to cakes for the feast. This is quite a ceremony in many households, as well as being the subject of music-hall jokes, for it is said that the women-folk always wish to make the traditional *kahk* and *ghorayyeba,* while the menfolk maintain that it is an unnecessary extravagance. It is customary for the different households to send samples of their festive fare to their neighbours and, of course, everybody is anxious to excel in her cooking and, also, to be the first to send her cakes. Towards the end of Ramadan, we see the huge trays of cakes for the feast on their way to the bakers' ovens, and perhaps some housewives may wish to know how they are made.

For the *ghorayyeba*—which is similar to a rich shortbread—you need half-an-oke of clarified butter, half-an-oke of castor sugar, and one oke of flour. The clarified butter must be beaten until white; then the sugar is added and the mixture beaten to a fine cream. When the flour is added, the mixture should be again well beaten and then divided up into small shapes ready for baking. The shapes are then garnished with blanched almonds and baked in a moderate oven.

The *kahk* is a little more complicated, and requires the preparation of a special filling called *'agameyya*. For this, about two spoonsful of sesame seeds are fried in butter, and a few spoonsful of flour rubbed into this. Three-quarters-of-a-pound of honey is added, and the mixture gently stirred before being removed from the fire.

For the *kahk*, you need an oke of flour, one-and-a-half pounds of clarified butter, and a pinch of salt. The butter is first warmed, then the flour rubbed in and the mixture left to cool. Warm water is then added to make a paste, which must be very well kneaded, and then again left to cool before the filling is added. The dough is moulded into small shapes, and an impression made in the centre into which the filling is placed. The dough is then folded back over the filling, and a pattern traced on the top of the shapes with a fork. The *kahk* is then baked in a moderate oven and, when cooked, should be dusted with powdered sugar.

Kahk and *ghorayyeba* are offered to visitors during the days of the Little Feast following Ramadan and, as visiting friends and relations is the custom at this time, one is likely to be called upon to sample a far greater number of these sweetmeats than is good for one. But anyway, the Little Feast, like Christmas, comes but once a year, and so one can cope with that extra piece of *kahk* in more or less the same spirit as one endures the extra piece of Christmas pudding or the additional mince pie! It is all part of the spirit of the feast—a time of rejoicing when we all wish each other the compliments of the season: *"Kol sana we entom tayyebeen!"* "Every year may you be well and happy!"

The Egyptian Gazette, June, 1953.

***

*Spend what is in your pocket
and what is in the unknown will come to you.*

PERSONAL REFLECTIONS

Hamati—my Egyptian Mother-in-Law

When I think about *Hamati*—which is Arabic for "my mother-in-law"—two pictures immediately come to mind. The first is a flashback to the scene some years ago when I arrived in Cairo to make my home there with my Egyptian husband. The whole family had turned out for the occasion—not just out of curiosity, but from a genuine desire to welcome the wife of a member of the family.

In Egypt and, I believe, in all countries of the Middle East, the family is a very real thing and shows little sign of splitting up and disintegrating under the influences of modern life. There is a saying in Egypt: "My brother and I against my cousin; my cousin and I against the stranger."

When I arrived, everyone was in black, because the old grandfather had just died and the family would be in mourning for some long time to come. *Hamati* was swathed in black, with the customary flimsy black headdress wound nun-wise over her head and under her chin, leaving only her round, unlined face visible, and her honey-coloured eyes gazing up into mine. She looked tiny and rather bewildered as she stood there beside me, and I myself could find no words to express my sentiments, for I had not yet learnt Arabic, and I had forgotten most of the conventional words of greeting in which my husband had schooled me. It was *Hamati* who first gained control of the situation, and she looked up earnestly into my face, patted my arm, and said a few words in this new, strange tongue. But the sweet smile which accompanied the words put me at my ease at once. "Mama welcomes you," translated my husband. "You will be to her like her own daughters."

The second picture which comes to mind when I think of *Hamati* is of a happy family gathering not long ago. The family circle had widened now, and there were new grandchildren running around and demanding attention. I was no longer a strange newcomer, but was one of the family group—laughing and chatting in a language which had by turns baffled and delighted me.

One of the best ways to get to understand a people is to study their proverbs and sayings, and I was always on the look-out for them when talking to my friends and relations. On this particular evening we were going over some Egyptian proverbs and comparing them with their English equivalents. "Have you got any sayings about mothers-in-law?" I asked. *Hamati* smiled. "Yes," she said. "There's an old one from the country, where most of the wise sayings come from. The peasants say: 'Your mother-in-law is a fever; your husband's sister is a poisonous scorpion, and your father-in-law is a snake behind the water-jar.' " How we all laughed at this, and mostly, I think, at the idea of *Hamati* telling this joke against herself. Not so long ago in Cairo they showed an Arabic film entitled *My Mother-in-law is an Atom Bomb!*

Some mothers-in-law may be considered as fevers or atom bombs, and *Hamati* is undeniably a very powerful influence and the whole family revolves around her. Most of her children are married now but, far from being deserted, the house is fuller than ever as the sons and daughters bring their wives and husbands and children home for care and advice. *Hamati* has never had much time for herself, and nowadays perhaps less than ever. There is always someone requiring her attention and the special kind of help she alone can give. When things have not been going so well with the family—when one member is in trouble or when some evil spirit seems to be exerting its influence—*Hamati* will embark on a procedure which might perhaps more nearly be described as a ritual. She will go down into one of the crowded bazaar quarters and purchase different kinds of incense—sandalwood, coriander, and frankincense—and let the fumes waft gently through the house, sweetening and purifying the air, and, *Hamati* believes, despatching the evil influences.

Then she will shut herself in the sitting-room, and soon the glow of candles may be seen through the frosted glass door. What form her ritual inside the room takes, noboby knows; but the subdued rhythm of prayer can be heard and, shortly afterwards, *Hamati* will emerge, candle in hand, with her white prayer *tarha* wrapped around her head and shoulders, and with an expression of contentment on her homely round face. These rites are exclusively her own—perhaps belonging in some way to Egypt's ancient past.

Yet withal, *Hamati* is a good practising Moslem. In the early morning, not long after dawn, she rises and performs her ablutions and, after making her first devotions of the day, she sits quietly reading the Qor'an until the house is astir and the everyday household duties begin to crowd once more upon her. She no longer observes the fast imposed upon Moslems during the month of Ramadan (her health would not permit of this ordeal) but, as usual, *Hamati* is easily the busiest member of the household: the fasters have to be looked after; there are guests to be entertained in the evening; there are the countless little charities in which she interests herself—particularly during this month—and, lastly, there are cakes and shortbreads to be made for the feast at the end of the month. Indeed, *Hamati* is busiest of all at feast-time. At the Big Feast, celebrated at the end of the Pilgrimage, she divides up the slaughtered sheep among the servants, the tradespeople, and the innumerable family retainers who have a strange habit of turning up at such moments!

It is to *Hamati* that we all turn at feast-time, at time of rejoicing and at time of sorrow. In time of sickness, she will be there with her special herb recipes for toothache, tummyache, eye-ache and headache; in time of family quarrels she will be giving her help and advice, dispensed with that knowledge and acceptance of the way of the world so characteristic of her.

Sometimes I ask *Hamati* what she would do if she suddenly had a windfall, if she won a lottery or sweepstake or something of the kind. She laughingly toys with the idea of building herself a house in the country and keeping her own poultry; or perhaps the notion of travel and visiting new lands interests her that day. And then she will sigh—rather a world-weary sigh, it seems to me. "But first I must make the Pilgrimage to Mecca," she says. "Now that my family has grown up and has no more need of me, I must allow myself a little time to please myself. Yes. To make the Pilgrimage. That is my dearest wish."

The Lady, London, February, 1964

***

Two Ladies of Eighty

Last year my mother celebrated her eightieth birthday, and this year my Egyptian mother-in-law followed suit. *Ma sha'Allah* for both of them—or, "As God wills," which is the Arabic way of saying "touch wood."

Completing their eightieth year would seem at first sight to be the only thing the two old ladies have in common. My mother has had a fairly adventurous life: rather go-ahead for her era, she went to college and qualified as a teacher, and then went to India as a Queen's Army school-mistress, where she met and married my father, who was serving there with an Irish regiment. Later on, when my sister and I were school age, her career took her to Hongkong, from where she made several trips to China and Japan. During the last war, she was serving in Singapore, and had to escape in hazardous-enough circumstances when the Japanese swept down the peninsula. She arrived back in England with only two suitcases in the world, to find the home she had stored in Plymouth had been completely destroyed by German bombs. But Mother has an optimistic nature, fortunately for all of us, and she was soon on her feet again, doing occupational therapy with the wounded soldiers until the end of the war, when my sister took her to live with her family on the outskirts of London.

My mother-in-law's life might seem uneventful. In a way, though, perhaps she was like my mother. At a time when there was no compulsory education in Egypt and all that was expected of a woman was to sit at home, sew a fine seam, then get married very young and have lots of children, *Hamati*—my mother-in-law—attended school up till the end of the preparatory stage. So, unlike many of her contemporaries, she could read and write Arabic and French. (Since Napoleon's Expedition in 1798 there had been a close cultural association between the two countries.) She married at twenty-three, late for that part of the world: the same age as my mother. Her husband, my father-in-law, was a Judge of Appeal, and with him she journeyed to different parts of Egypt—to Alexandria, to towns in the Delta and others in Upper Egypt. In this way, like my mother, she never stayed long in any one place, and after a few years the home would have to be packed up and moved to new quarters, with the consequent knocking-about suffered by the furniture—still in evidence today! When the children were born—she had eight, with six now surviving—*Hamati* did like my mother and went home to Mum. Here, any similarity would probably end: while my sister and I were duly christened some six weeks or so after birth, *Hamati*'s offspring were given a *seboo'* party on the seventh day following their entry into the world, with prayers and songs, with beating of drums and rattling of tin trays and all kinds of noises that you would think would scare a baby out of its wits but by which they seem surprisingly unaffected. There are gifts for the child at this time—a miniature golden Qor'an on a chain, turquoise-studded bracelets and ear-rings to keep away the evil-eye, and little silver mugs like those given to children here at Christening. Again, quite unlike in England, my mother-in-law's first-born (who became my husband!) was immediately appropriated by the grandmother, as was frequently the custom in those days. His brothers and sisters, however, moved about with their parents in Egypt as my sister and I did when our parents had to go abroad.

Both of my old ladies have been widowed a long time: my mother for over thirty years and my mother-in-law for fifteen. I remember both the deaths—not so different, for Death is the great leveller. The nuns were praying around my father's bedside when we arrived at the nursing-home where he had been since his stroke, while at my father-in-law's death-bed the sheikh stood chanting from the Holy Qor'an. My father's flag-covered coffin made its slow last journey in a black hearse, while my father-in-law's was borne shoulder-high to the mosque by self-appointed bearers—male members of the family, friends, family retainers, and local tradesmen taking it in turns.

My mother and mother-in-law have both been fortunate in not being lonely in their old age. Up till a few years ago, *Hamati* had one or other of her sons with his family living with her: now, she has a grandson to stay in her flat, while every day members of the family call on her, and at feast time—at the end of the fasting month of Ramadan, at Moslem New Year, and at the Feast of the Pilgrimage, she is still the centre of the picture. All her family come first to her house to greet her in the traditional way: *Kol sana w' enti tayyeba":* "May you be well and happy every year." My mother, too, living with my sister, is not lonely in her later years, although, living in

Egypt, I can manage to see her only during my summer vacation.

When my mother came on holiday to Egypt, she used to visit *Hamati*, and the two of them would sit together, smiling and nodding at each other, but unable to converse because of the difference in language. I used to think then they were strangely alike—the smartly-dressed, much-travelled Western career woman and the homely Oriental matron, with her black mourning *tarha* wound about her rather shapeless form. They had both seen their families grow up, lost their husbands, had the joy of grandchildren, and now both were content to sit back and philosophically watch the world go by. Kipling's adage about East and West may be true up to a point, but it seems to me that the twain start together and then meet again, somewhere towards the end of the road.

B.B.C. "Home this Afternoon," 1969

* * *

He whom God loves He made to be loved by others.

* * *

Teaching English on Two Sides of the Nile

Teaching English on two sides of the River Nile is not just a matter of greeting colleagues and students with "Hello" instead of "Hi," and spelling "traveller" with two "l"s rather than one. It is all this, and a great deal more.

In the first place, one might ask how a situation could arise where one found oneself teaching British English on the west bank of the Nile and the American variety on the east. The answer is simple: the British Council is located on the west side, on Nile Road, and I have been teaching English there during their summer session. My regular job, however, is at the American University in Cairo, situated over the other side of the Nile, in Liberation Square. The Freshman Writing Program where I teach does not offer courses during the summer, requiring as they do a full semester, whereas the AUC summer session is only six weeks. The British Council,

132

meanwhile, has introduced summer courses for the first time, and I was pleased to have the opportunity of participating in them.

The change proved interesting and stimulating. For two "modules," one of six weeks, the other three, I was teaching grammar, reading, and aural comprehension to intermediate-level students, instead of teaching writing to freshmen. The groups from the British Council were a little larger than those of the American University, numbering about twenty students, compared with fifteen at the university. The first British Council group was of teachers from technical schools, preparing for courses in Britain, and representing a wide variety of subjects—agricultural engineering, machine knitting, machine-made garments, soil conservation and animal husbandry—to name only a few. The group for the intensive summer-school course of three weeks numbered about twenty-four students, some new and some continuing from the lower level. This was the first time the British Council Language Centre had run a summer school, and there was a big response, with many students having to be turned away. The elementary and intermediate courses accommodated some three hundred students in fifteen classes of twenty each. These were concurrent with two Temporary Registration Assessment Board courses for doctors preparing to go to Britain for further study.

A course in the appreciation of literature was also offered by the British Council during the summer, to find out whether any demand existed for such a course. Those registering included some literature students from Cairo University, Mass Communications graduates, and a few literature enthusiasts. Contributions to the course were made by a number of summer-school teachers, and included many different subjects in the genre. There appeared to be an enthusiastic response to the course, and the Language Centre hopes to include similar ones in future.

Teaching English on the west bank of the Nile instead of the east during the summer provided matter for reflection not only so far as difference in methods, subjects and accent were concerned. The British Council Language Centre and the American University are both within walking distance of my home on the island of Zamalek, but whereas the walk to the university is through Gezira Club and over the main bridge of Qasr el Nil to Liberation Square, the British Council is reached from my home by way of Zamalek

Bridge over the smaller branch of the river. On the west bank of *Agouza*—"Old Woman"—once were fertile fields, villages, orchards, and flower nurseries; even now, although the area is built up as far as the eye can see right to the Pyramids, some agricultural areas remain. On the walk to the British Council at 8.15 a.m., there were peasants to be seen, bringing in their produce to market; women in their long, yoked gowns walked gracefully along together, chattering brightly, and carrying great copper bowls of cream cheese on their heads and sometimes a couple of ducks in a wicker basket, while cyclists passed by with their carriers piled high with summer blooms—tuberoses and delphiniums. Zamalek is a busy suburb of flats, villas, and shops, but over on the west side one is nearer to the country people of Egypt, whereas on the east side one is in the town, leading to the old settlement of Cairo.

In October, I shall be back teaching writing at the American University, refreshed by the many changes experienced in teaching English on the other side of the Nile.

IATEFL Newsletter, October, 1978

***

Hidden alms is in buying and selling.

***

My two homes in Egypt and England

Twenty-five years ago I sailed away one blustery March day to start my life in Egypt with my Egyptian husband. Since then, I've come to look on London and Cairo as my two homes. In fact, the other day when my hairdresser asked me whether my hair became drier "at home," I had to think for a moment or two where he was referring to: I suppose in some ways this dichotomy is a bad thing—not knowing where you really belong. But I think it is inevitable when one marries a foreigner and for me its great advantage has been to give me a very keen appreciation of both countries and both ways of life: much more so than if I had never gone away for more than an annual holiday.

I've mentioned my homes in London and Cairo, but I don't actually live right in the centre of either capital. In England, I live on the outskirts of London, in the "green belt" on the fringe of Epping Forest; in Egypt, I have to cross one of the branches of the Nile to get to my home on the large island or *Gezira* which separates Lower Egypt and the Delta from Upper Egypt—Giza and Luxor. As you can imagine, nothing could be more different than these two places: in England I have the woods at my doorstep, and I can roam for hours over the common, picking hawthorn blossom, wild roses or blackberries. In Egypt, I can go picnicking in the desert, riding on horseback or camel, and perhaps seeing some of the latest excavations in the pyramids area. Just outside London, my family have a delightful garden with flowers blooming at almost any time of year: in Cairo, most of us live in flats and not many people are fortunate enough to have gardens. Instead, there are parks and public gardens, and for some of us there are clubs where we can play tennis all the year round and swim on the hot summer days. There are no open fields in Egypt where you can laze in the sun, because the narrow strip of fertile land on either side of the Nile is needed for intensive cultivation. But trees have been planted everywhere in the valley, along the river banks, beside the irrigation canals and on either side of the road, giving shade and beauty. In summertime, the cassia trees are in bloom, delicate pink and vivid "flame of the forest," while in spring the willows wave their delicate fronds beside the river. In England, the first thing we notice when we are on holiday is the greenness everywhere; but the summer scene in Cairo is a brilliant one, with the intensely blue sky, and the white sails of felukas on the Nile, the green of the flame trees and the red carpet of their blossoms. There are plenty of tourists in Egypt in the summer nowadays—not like the last century, when it was just a winter resort for the idle rich! I think people like a change from every-day routine, whether in scene, food or climate.

One of the main reasons why I'm happy whether living in Cairo or London is that I'm near a great river in both cases. Just now, we're not so near the Thames, it's true, but in the days before I went to Egypt I used to live and work in London, and to walk along by the river or just to gaze out over it when crossing by train or bus gave me the same feeling of peace that I get in Egypt when I'm near the Nile. I have to cross over it every day on my way to the American University, where I work as a teacher of English as a foreign language—teaching mainly Arabic-speaking students the intricacies of English! Like the Thames, the Nile is a truly wonderful river, and always changing in its mood and aspect. In winter-time, it is usually tranquil, like the picture-postcards you see of it, with white-sailed felukas reflected in its waters. But then suddenly a wild wind lashes its surface and the river is transformed into a sea, with white horses riding the waves. At this time of the year, before the building of the High Dam at Aswan, the appearance of the Nile used to change completely, with the turbulent brown waters of the annual flood swirling and eddying past, and at the same time reflecting the brilliant blue sky. I for one am really sorry there's no more Nile flood. I found this one of the most fascinating and romantic things about Egypt when I first went there and it was one of the first things I wrote about in my writings on Egyptian life and customs. You know, the annual flood had been going on for thousands upon thousands of years—"from time immemorial" as nearly every Egyptian school-child writes in his essay, and he quotes the Greek historian Herodotus, who proclaimed that "Egypt is the gift of the Nile." And the Pharaoh Akhenaton, husband of Nefertiti, wrote a poem to his One God, expressing his gratitude for the great river and the flood. As I said before, all these romantic associations of the Nile absolutely fascinated me when I went to live in Egypt, and I felt myself very fortunate to be living near the river, as I had been in England. Somehow, it was a common factor that made the transition from one way of life to another much smoother. Not all foreign women who married Egyptians were so fortunate, though; many found they had to settle in a desert suburb like that of Heliopolis—"City of the Sun," where they're far away from the Nile, with its palms and weeping willows and heavily-laden river-craft. They got used to it for the most part, though, and enjoyed the dry desert air and the cooler summer nights. And, of course, not everybody feels the same way as I about living near a river!

But so much has changed both in London and Cairo since I went to Egypt a quarter of a century ago that I'm really not speaking about the same places when I talk about my homes here and there. Every time I come back to London, there have been changes, and not always small ones: all the new buildings and the great blocks that have gone up everywhere, the increased number of immigrants, the single-decker red London buses, to name only a few. In Cairo it's the same: probably the biggest change has been in the population—the huge numbers of people you see everywhere. We have no underground system in Cairo,* though, and to cope with the pedestrian problem in the centre of the city, an extended overpass has been built to keep the roads clear for the great mass of traffic. And then there's the change in the people themselves: most of the cosmopolitan population that dominated the capital in the days before the 1952 Revolution has disappeared, and nowadays it's mostly Arabic you hear spoken, rather than Levantine French, Italian and Greek. And of course there's a huge increase in the industrial working-class and far fewer long *galabeyya* robes worn by the men, or black sheet-like swathes by the women, though there are still a few diehards like my one-time home-help who would have considered it a disgrace to appear in a dress or blouse and skirt in the street. (But, as a sign of the times, she's recently got herself a pensionable job as nurse-orderly in a new hospital!) Then, by way of change in the city itself, there are the fine new roads and buildings and the Cairo Tower, like London's Post Office Tower, but in lotus leaf design to fit in with the pharaonic scene.

Another aspect of my life in London and Cairo that's inevitably changed enormously is that of my family, both here and there. When I first went to Egypt, I lived with my in-laws, as many people still do, though the custom is dying out. Both my father-in-law and mother-in-law were still alive and there was a sister-in-law and two of my husband's brothers still at home, unmarried. I learnt a tremendous amount about the Egyptian way of life through my contact with them. They all gave me a wonderfully warm welcome when I first arrived, my mother-in-law assuring me that I'd be "like her own daughter." Although she spoke no English, and I knew no Arabic at that time, she did a lot to help me become integrated in this new and strange society. Of course, we didn't always get on so well together, and there were the usual difficulties and jealousies inherent in such a situation, but we both admired and respected each other. She and my own mother died last year, both in their early eighties, and I miss them both terribly. The Egyptians have an expression of condolence: "The blessing now comes from you," and I can understand this now that these two old ladies are gone: the older generation has passed, and now it is we who carry the

---

* One is being built now   1984

burden and are the givers, not receivers. My old father-in-law died a long time ago: through him I'd been able to catch a glimpse of the old world of the landed class in Egypt. He was the eldest member of the extended family and in retirement he used to manage the land, giving advice on crops and the like, so I came to understand a lot about agricultural Egypt.

My husband and I met during the war when we were working in broadcasting, and I've kept up my broadcasting interests and friends over the years. More recently I took up teaching: it's the ideal profession if you have children, and by now I had a daughter demanding my time and attention. At first, I taught English language and literature at a girls' secondary school—which my daughter now attends. It was at this time, I think, that I became very much aware of the difference in my two homes in England and Egypt, and to wonder where I really belonged. I hadn't noticed this so much when I was still working in broadcasting, because that was very much the same in both places. But when I had to teach English poetry of the Romantic period and try to explain Keats' "Ode to Autumn," I was really up against it! How was I to explain to my Egyptian pupils the way in England the leaves turned red and gold in autumn, and how the earth slept under a blanket of snow in winter? Because in Egypt there's practically no "fall," no wild west wind to scatter the leaves, and in winter the land is green with crops, not white with snow.

In fact, I don't think this problem of "which *is* home?" can, or need, ever be settled. Both England and Egypt, London and Cairo, mean a tremendous lot to me: England is my native land, where I grew up and went to school, and London is where I had my first jobs. Egypt is the setting for my married life, and my daughter was born in Cairo. Both London and Cairo have their own individual beauty and fascinating history. And whether I'm arriving in London and being met by my family and friends or landing in Cairo at the end of my holiday, the greeting I get is the same: *Ahlan w' sahlan:* "Welcome Home."

B.B.C. "Woman's Hour," 1971

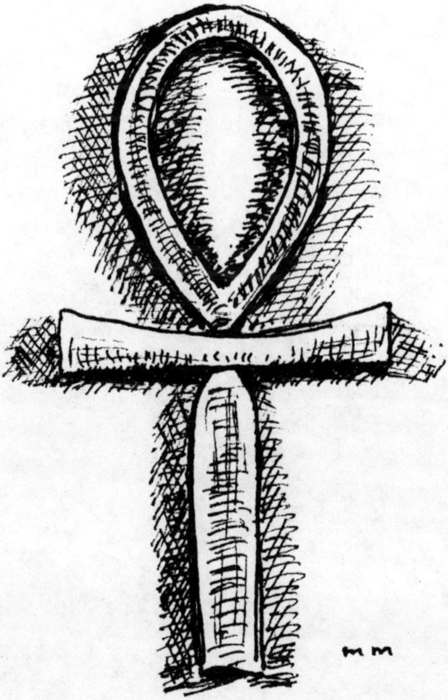

Produced by the Printshop of the American University in Cairo Press